After Pestilence

After Pestilence

An Interreligious Theology of the Poor

Mario I. Aguilar

scm press

© Mario I. Aguilar 2021

Published in 2021 by SCM Press
Editorial office
3rd Floor, Invicta House,
108–114 Golden Lane,
London EC1Y OTG, UK
www.scmpress.co.uk

SCM Press is an imprint of Hymns Ancient & Modern Ltd
(a registered charity)

Hymns Ancient & Modern® is a registered trademark of
Hymns Ancient & Modern Ltd
13A Hellesdon Park Road, Norwich,
Norfolk NR6 5DR, UK

British Library Cataloguing in Publication data
A catalogue record for this book is available
from the British Library

978-0-33406-035-2

Typeset by Regent Typesetting
Printed and bound by
CPI Group (UK) Ltd

Contents

Dedicated to Glenda Tello

Acknowledgements

This book came out of the shock, the trauma and the isolation of the global Covid-19 pandemic that began in 2020. As I couldn't return to Scotland from Chile, I realized that the BBC and other journalists were asking me to react, to feel the developments of the pandemic and to provide thoughts, prayers and actions for others who were in shock as well. Years ago, I had rejected the notion that I could be an interlocutor for liberation theology and the poor because over the past 26 years I have been cosily reading and writing at the Faculty of Theology of the University of St Andrews. Suddenly, and as the days passed by in quiet quarantine, the solidarity of the poor around me and the quiet breeze of the Lord's silence started transforming such past thought. As my hair grew longer and 143 days passed in the flat without going out, I understood that liberation theology and interreligious dialogue had a lot to do with each other in the life of the marginalized who pulled together to provide food and shelter to the very poor. The poor looked after me at all times, making sure that I behaved like the one they wanted: a quiet older man who could make sense of what God was saying in those moments. Their understanding was metaphysical: if my writing and my prayers would cease, they would get ill; if I could protect them with my brief appearance they would survive. In the midst of such turmoil, workers asked me about the Dalai Lama, and Jesuits ran through the streets nearby with encouragement for migrants and harsh words towards the government. Only one resident of our building died of the virus and six of us were put on a list of those vulnerable who would follow. In those moments, I prayed, I wrote and I poured issues of social justice and interreligious solidarity to the foreign media.

I dedicate this book to my life companion, who with courage was my anchor to hope and heaven during those months, as always. My life companion, who was elsewhere in the city, made sure that I would not fail to look after myself with an infinite hope that everything would be all right. Like Hildegard: *Quadam in visione beatorum in paradiso animas contemplator Hildegard, quae exspectant ut suis corporibus coniungantur.*

On the completion of this book Dom Pedro Casaldáliga, bishop, poet and theologian of liberation, died in Brazil (August 2020) while I was in quarantine. His life inspired many of us and I realized how he was a remarkable prophet of the Kingdom, who even prepared his own food and washed his clothes by hand. He was a poet who poured revolution and Eucharist all together in whatever he did. When he died, I went to the streets and told those around me that this was the chance to pray for the intercession of Dom Pedro so that the sick would be healed and the bereaved would be consoled. A new saint had arrived in heaven – St Pedro Casaldáliga of the Amazonia, pray for us!

I am grateful to those who accompanied this writing from other continents and showed their unfailing support, especially Sara Aguilar, Dr Eve Parker, Dr James Morris and Dr Ann Simpson. My gratitude to Dr Gordon Barclay for the hope of having dinner together again, and to the following who commented on this work and reminded me of their companionship: Carolina Sanz, the Revd Dr Webster Siame Kameme, Braulia Ribeiro, Kabir Babu, Porsiana Beatrice, Marjorie Gourlay, Matyas Bodi, Stefanie Knecht, Hunter Daggett, Gillian Chu, Isaac Portilla and Emilie Krenn-Grosvenor.

In Santiago city centre a dozen young immigrants from Venezuela, and Chilean workers at the building where I stayed, looked after me to the point that I was a prisoner of their caution and their encouragement to have eggs and cakes and to remain in my flat while the sick, the infirm and the dying were being taken by ambulances from all these buildings. Particular thanks to Daniela Vidal, a courageous Chilean mother who symbolized the solidarity of the marginalized during the pandemic. Particular thanks to the Vatican press office and civil service who managed to provide every possible document I needed and cleared all materials needed to assess the important role of Pope Francis during the pandemic. My gratitude to friends at the St Mary's College office who kept me alert and cared for at a distance. To Edna Adan and friends in Hargeisa, Somaliland, thanks for weekly exchanges on developments in Somaliland, and for your example of fortitude and order during the pandemic.

Finally, a word of appreciation to the Fellows and members of Laudato Si' International and to members of the Milarepa Foundation, particularly Ivonne Bell, Jorge Cuché, Marcela Arévalo and Dr Camila Foncea. To my fellow Knights, Christians and Muslims, Peace! *Non nobis, Domine, non nobis, sed Nomini tuo da gloriam!*

Santiago, Chile,
August 2020

Introduction
A Post-Pandemic Theology of
Interfaith Liberation

'We are living among the dead', an intensive care medical doctor who had already battled for ten weeks from the start of the pandemic in Chile told us. It was May 2020 and this shocking proposition had already been outlined by those experiencing the Covid-19 pandemic in China and Europe but not in Latin America. Massive contagion and cases started appearing later, and the media did not show the medical consequences of the pandemic until much later. Thus, sensorial acute shock had not entered the emotional spaces of human fear. Those who had reacted already to the danger and to the global fear had been those Catholics and members of other faith communities who had been invited by Pope Francis to join him online on 27 March to pray for the City of Rome and for the world.[1] Theologically, that was the moment when Pope Francis, the global parish priest, represented the priest of the communal sacrifice. He prayed to the sacrificial Christ on the cross for the end of the pandemic on behalf of all: spare your people, Lord! Spare your people! – a real 'tempest alone' that was reported as far as Thailand.[2]

For memory and sensorial experience are two different experiences, so they can be compared to the difference between two types of contemporary theologies, one rational and philosophical (European), the other experiential and contextual (within the southern hemisphere).[3] One can study, outline and reflect theologically on the past, be it the Christian incarnation or the Spanish flu, but to experience such incarnation is

1

different.[4] The foundations of the Eucharist, for example, can be thought with an inbuilt sense of the tradition and with clear questions about what happened in Jerusalem when Jesus took bread and wine and shared supper with his disciples.[5] The other kind of theological experience carries in its methodology a theological 'after thought' in which the moment of action and the post-reflection become closely intertwined simply because the action and the reaction are closely related.[6] This was the case, for example, with the Eucharist celebrated by Archbishop Oscar Romero in which he was killed on 24 March 1980 in San Salvador.[7] Romero's last homilies, taken as his theological reflections within political theology, got him killed. If one were to speak of liberating moments of martyrdom and sacrifice, the killing of Romero, of the Jesuit Rutilio Grande and companions, as well as Ignacio Ellacuría and companions in El Salvador, have been deemed martyrdoms and an offering for others by the Church.[8] Not only did they reflect theologically and publicly on the events that affected the Christian communities in El Salvador, but when Ignacio Ellacuría and companions were machined-gunned, such a moment became a moment of sensorial social shock followed by memory, rather than the other way around.[9]

Memory and sensorial hermeneutical actions have influenced the development of contextual theologies outside Europe, and the immanent relations of an inter-hybridity between theologies of the world religions and the politics attached to such dialogue in situ, in society, at the local and extra-ecclesial level, are deemed significant.[10] Indeed, the foundations of political theology, as critiqued by Peterson, already outlined 'monotheism as a political problem' simply because the ancients used the concept of a single divinity in order to justify monarchical powers.[11] However, the foundations of political theology did not follow the rational possibilities of a unified ideology but argued for a diverse possibility based on the ongoing experience of people.[12] Indeed, Metz' theology as a European predecessor of Latin American political theologies argued strongly that memory, solidarity and narrative turn theological attention to the 'dangerous memory of Jesus Christ', and the *anamnesis* becomes central to memory in the Eucharist.[13] Thus, Metz' reworking of all Christian theology through the Holocaust made him into a theologian who not only understood the disruptive experience of the Holocaust but actually integrated history – real history, not only an interpretation of history – into his theology of compassion.[14] The compassion of God is actualized through a sensitivity for the suffering of others, and a passion for God.[15] Metz became a source for liberation theology in its use of history, and becomes a source-cum-memory for our own compassion for humanity and for an emphatic ethical behaviour for human beings in history during the pandemic.[16] However, where there is compassion there is context, and where there is context there is the presence of God so that theologizing takes place in a particular context.

Context becomes the place where God acts and where God manifests herself, while theological books are places where we inscribe our experience of God, and that in the case of the biblical text becomes a nourishing and salvific event for later generations.[17] If sickness is a human experience and therefore a shared universal experience, the experience of secluded extra-wall lepers or cancer patients in hospital today can became a human experience that we can comprehend but we have not experienced.[18] Indeed, lockdown or isolation are experiences that have triggered a sensorial and conceptual locality and historicity towards a pandemic, towards an experience of the plague that we have read in books but seemed to have disappeared because of the so-called 'triumph' of science. Hermeneutical and theological knowledge thus becomes complementary to the medical knowledge of the pandemic, simply because social isolation becomes a must and a reason not to interact with others in ways that have been fostered during the twentieth century.

What emerged in 2020 was a sickness, a contagious sickness of global proportions, for which we did not have a vaccine, medication or a cure. Further, leprosy in the New Testament is an experience of isolation, in which the sick person is taken away and families forbidden from visiting, while those who die of such sickness are taken away in a closed casket and buried quickly with very little contact with other human beings. It is the experience not only of lepers in the past but also the experience of Jesus of Nazareth, a political outcast condemned to death and therefore buried without major festivals or signals. That problem becomes our problem, and the problem of Mary in John 20.2: 'they have taken the Lord and we do not know where they have put him'. How can we do theology in a situation of death and massive death? And what kind of theology can be outlined within such time and space? Is God present in such a pandemic?

None of these questions are new and we have the experience of Israel leaving Egypt, Israel within the exile and return, Jesus being killed on a cross, the disciples going from Jerusalem to Rome, and the martyrs in Rome and elsewhere. But foremost we have our own experience of military regimes, martyrs such as St Oscar Romero, the Jesuits of El Salvador, martyrs of civil wars and natural disasters, and martyrs of interfaith dialogue such as Charles de Foucault.[19] We are prepared within faith and the tradition for a full reflection on history and Christian witness but we are not fully prepared for a twenty-first-century reflection on a global response to suffering. And this is what has changed: Christian theology operates within a globalized theology of the poor and the marginalized, and a response that now unites reflections by different Christian traditions as well as the response of Judaism, Islam, Buddhism, Hinduism, Jainism, African religions and many other contemporary traditions of faith in the beyond. Such interreligious and communal action of solidarity has provoked a response to a material world which is limited. A world that understands science and religion as explanations of a journey has come of age, not through a sectarian response but through the production and the utterance of shared narratives about God. Those narratives are central to the human responses to a global journey in which God is one of us and in which God is present in each human being we encounter now and throughout a journey after pestilence.

It could be argued, and I do so within this work, that what we have experienced in the context of Covid-19 is a theology of the dead. Christianity has provided an orderly and clean passage from birth to death, and a global sickness has challenged such order with no open churches, no sacraments at hand and no lineal precision, without our control, 'strange times', and without an end. It is my argument that, as happened previously, we have been asked to serve neighbour and God, but in our theological reflection we must realize that a new theological period has begun. Previously, there were periods of theological and indeed ecclesial *aggiornamento* that brought theology into contact with the poor and the marginalized and through which contextual theology rediscovered its roots in the early Church. Theologically we developed a different avatar of God, a God that was metaphorically poor with us, but during the pandemic such a God became a true reality in which theologizing was done within a situation of fear and a real danger of contagion.

One can return to that period of Vatican II (1962–65) and after the call by John XXIII for a 'Church of the poor', to find a moment when there was a definition of the Church as interested in the joys and sadness of all humans, rather than only those who were baptized, and baptized within a single Christian tradition, even within a majority Christian tradition.[20] The response to the question, 'Church, who are you'? was a direct response to the central question of all theistic religions, 'Who is God?' A natural response to the centrality of Europe came challenging colonialism and secularism but the surprising and challenging responses came from Latin America, the continent where more Christians lived, followed by the association between such reflection with the comparative theological and contextual questions by Africans, Asians, women, those in the LGBT community, transgenders and indigenous populations.[21]

The effects of an initial dialogue with the world that had been emphasized and systematized by Vatican II had a deep impact in Latin America, a continent where the majority of Christians of the world live.[22] The *aggiornamento* that took place in Latin America did not have an impact on conferences or world meetings on dialogue but shaped very quickly a refreshed mode of being church, a model from below in which everybody was able to feel at home in the Church and the world, particularly through the so-called Basic Ecclesial Communities (CEB).[23] The first characteristics of dialogue with the world that *Gaudium et Spes* had emphasized were realized in the 1968 meeting of Latin American bishops in Medellin (Colombia) and the subsequent 'preferential option for the poor' declared by the Latin American bishops against all pressures by the Vatican in Puebla de los Angeles (Mexico) in 1979.[24]

The main thrust of this renewal, of what I have elsewhere called 'a new reformation' in Latin America, came through a rethinking of theological paradigms associated with dogmatic statements and a new reading of history.[25] Within this new theological reading effected by a materialistic reading of history, the 'people of God', in their majority poor and their history, became closer to the people of Israel and the Israelites at the time of Jesus, living in societies full of conflict, violence, poverty and suffering.[26] I have argued for the acknowledgement of this theological leap for the poor within history in other contexts and particularly within a situation of extreme violence such as the Rwanda genocide of 1994.[27] In that work I emphasized the place of justice in dialogue, rather than reconciliation and forgetting, arguing that the dialogue with the world religions starts from the realization that human beings living in poverty and uncertainty have a central place in the theological narratives about God, that is, 'the victims of globalization are part of larger symbolic globalized communities; namely, the world religions'.[28] Theologizing with the poor in liberation and together with world religions becomes the only plausibility for the Kingdom of God and within the Beatitudes during the twenty-first century because the poor *are* the presence of God and the first sacramental presence of the Divinity in the process of theologizing.

Theology as a Second Act

For Gutiérrez, theology is a second act and a narrative that uses language in order to understand God's presence in the world. Thus, for Gutiérrez, 'Theology is a language. It attempts to speak a word about the mysterious reality that believers call God. It is a *logos* about *theos*.'[29] Theology is not a first act for a theologian; the first act is clearly faith, expressed in prayer and commitment within the Christian community.[30] However, that clear statement had been the product of many years of theological disputes, doctrinal misunderstandings, interpretative projects, engagement with Marxists and neo-liberals, and all within a changing Latin American Church that became fully engaged with the world of politics, economics and development.[31] In other words, for Gutiérrez, theology is a textual narrative that arises out of a practice within a particular context of a Christian community engaged with the world, and particularly within the world of the poor and the disadvantaged of society.[32]

It is clear that Gutiérrez' treatment of religion and politics presupposes God's presence in human history through a Church engaged with the world, in which it is necessary to participate actively in the political in order to act religiously. Religion as the ritual and social practices of a rule of life (*religio*) produces theology as a narrative. That narrative as a text allows practitioners (and others) to follow historical interpretations of the rule of life, and those interpretations also affect the way in which practitioners understand practices within that way of life. Therefore, and according to Gutiérrez, religion and politics are embodied in religious ritual and secular governance respectively through a constant dialectic of interaction, contradiction and solidarity.

It is in that response to religious practice in the contemporary world of the 1960s and within that framework of a *post-idealist theology* that Metz and Gutiérrez independently articulated a theological narrative that described and challenged the possibility of theologizing outside the social structures of political governance and indeed of people's lives.[33] Metz' context is European and he developed a strong political theology, while Gutiérrez' context is Latin America (and the third world) and he develops a theological framework known as liberation theology.[34] For both theologians religion and politics are not separate entities; instead they come out of actions carried out by Christians who involve themselves with those in need within society, involvement that arises from their religious selfhood and their Christian life in community. The place of the Church in history is not as establishment but as people, and the place of theology is of narrative rather than doctrine.

The influence of those ideas was enormous in Catholic theological circles not because those were new ideas (it must be remembered that the social doctrine of the Church had been articulated since 1891) but because they were the first theological fruits of Vatican II. The 'post-idealist' narrative of God's work in the world had returned to the biblical and doctrinal sources that had been confused by European philosophical epistemologies within European theology. The works of Metz in Europe and of Gutiérrez in Latin America became catalysts for pastoral models centred on the concept of the 'people of God' rather than on the Church as the only place where God could or should intervene within the contemporary world.

Gutiérrez' talk to a group of priests in Chimbote, Peru, in 1968 and the subsequent publication of his seminal work did not end theological discussions on pastoral matters related to the implementation of Vatican II but activated a clear theological exploration of the place of religious practitioners within society.[35] The European context of secularism and atheism was changed into a theological narrative that explored the religious practices and beliefs of Christians within a heavily religious environment that questioned the political governance offered within their own societies. Theological works spoke of the 'irruption of the poor', of oppressors and oppressed, of liberation from personal sin as well as from sinful structures of governance ('structural sin').

The impact of Gutiérrez' work was enormous because he relocated a majestic God with a triumphant Church into an anthropomorphic and incarnate deity closer to the Hebrew Scriptures than to Greek thought and platonic ideals. The rediscovery of the Scriptures as authority within the Catholic Church at Vatican II helped to question the possible dichotomies of the neo-scholastics by returning to the Old Testament where a daily interaction included religious practices. Within such social practice there was no clear separation between religion and politics because religion and *religio* were part of the daily life of a society. North American and European theologians took Gutiérrez' challenge and organized conferences and seminars in order to examine their own theological presuppositions and the diversified contexts in which those theological statements were being made. The students of the University of Chicago, for example, organized a conference in 1979 where the new Shailer Matthews Professor of Divinity, Langdon Gilkey, addressed their concerns with the following statement.

Surely there can be no doubt that the important later symbols of the New Covenant people, the messianic reign, and even the Kingdom itself repeat and develop, rather than abrogate, this union of the social and the religious, the historical and the ideal, which begins here in the original calling and establishment of the people of God. This interrelation and interdependence of the religious and the social, the individual and the communal – and the providential constitution of both was re-expressed in classical, Hellenistic form in Augustine's *De Civitate Dei*, and variously – and often unfortunately – in the subsequent concepts of Holy Christendom and in the Calvinistic views of the Holy Community.[36]

Within Latin America, Africa and Asia, theologians explored their commitment, their religious practices and the political world in which they lived. Within North America the oppressed of the past and of the present asked questions about their role in society (their religion), God's involvement in the world (their theology), and their politicians' governance of society (their politics). However, while most theologians, academics and politicians have explored some of Gutiérrez' ideas related to his first period of work, he continued his practice of religion and his ministry as a priest in a slum of Lima, where the politics of Peruvian society required him to reflect on his practice through two other research periods: one on the place of history in God's plan of salvation, and another one on the place of political events and the teaching of the Church as its response. Gutiérrez found a companion in the anthropologist, novelist and poet José María Arguedas (1911–69), who wrote about the poor and challenged the oppression towards the poor within Peruvian society. They met at Chimbote, a coastal fishing port to the north of Lima, while Gutiérrez was giving conferences and Arguedas was finishing his novel *El zorro de arriba y el zorro de abajo*.[37] Arguedas influenced Gutiérrez and vice versa, because both found that God was present in the poor of Peru, either in Chimbote or in Rimac, a Lima slum where Gutiérrez ministered through a parish and through his Las Casas Institute.[38] It is difficult to imagine but it was at the Rimac slum that Gutiérrez wrote most of his theology, teaching only part-time at the university.[39]

Theology as History

If during his first theological period Gutiérrez asked questions about social and divine processes of underdevelopment and poverty, during his second period of research he asked questions about God's involvement in human history.[40] Gutiérrez' understanding of human history followed Vatican II in its document on the Church in the modern world, where the Council Fathers asserted, 'The Lord is the goal of human history, the focal point of the desires of history and civilization, the centre of mankind, the joy of all hearts, and the fulfilment of all aspirations.'[41] Those thoughts had been applied to the Latin American pastoral reality in Gutiérrez' seminal talk to the meeting of the National Office for Social Research in Chimbote (July 1968) when he stated:

> If there is a finality inscribed in history, then the essence of Christian faith is to believe in Christ, that is to believe that God is irreversibly committed to human history. To believe in Christ, then, is to believe that God has made a commitment to the historical development of the human race. To have faith in Christ is to see the history in which we are living as the progressive revelation of the human face of God.[42]

His main source for this second period was the biblical text, and he argued for one major theological presupposition: God became human through the incarnation and therefore he became one of us. The outcome of such a theological presupposition is that God acts through human history in order to save and he administers graces for human beings in order to interact in the world and be part of it. As a result, religious practice (religion) takes place within a particular society that is governed not by others but by the same 'people of God', with the Church as a community immersed in a particular society. However, that incarnation as theological principle was relevant to the people of Israel in the Old Testament. Yahweh led his people out of oppression at an early stage of their history, he gave them the land and he asked them to keep a covenant that included just and equal relations between all. Within those just relations the prophets reminded Israel of her obligations towards the poor, the needy, the widows, the orphans and the stranger.[43] The demands by God in the history of Israel point to the fact that 'the history from which biblical faith springs is an open-ended history, a history open to the future'.[44]

Gutiérrez moved to a rereading of Latin American history by assuming God's involvement in human history throughout the Hebrew Scriptures. The history of Latin America was no different from that of Israel because within that human history there were God-fearing people who asked questions about history in order to understand questions about God. If the liberation of Israel through the Exodus made a people, Gutiérrez explored the 'encounter' between Europeans and indigenous peoples in 1492. Christians led a colonial conquest based initially on ideals of civilization and evangelization but was subsequently driven by human greed and an ongoing strife for riches and power.[45] Those who suffered poverty and social annihilation under the conquistadors became part of a society that proclaimed itself Christian and in the name of an unjust Christian relation between colonizers and colonized subjected indigenous peoples to slavery, genocide, forced conversion and inhuman conditions of life.[46] Nevertheless, for Gutiérrez, God was in Latin America in pre-Columbian times and he remained with the suffering indigenous peoples while many atrocities were taking place.

In reading Latin American history Gutiérrez isolated the example of some Christians who did not comply with the status quo of colonialism and degradation and became themselves defenders of the poor for the sake of the gospel. One of them, Bartolomé de las Casas, was an example of a full conversion to the poor in colonial Latin America, who allowed his voice to be heard within the Spanish Courts and the learned universities of Europe.[47] Las Casas' attitude and his Christian attitude made a difference in God's action in history because he defended the poor and the needy, and in return he became a sign of contradiction who had to suffer attacks from philosophers, theologians and conquistadors alike.[48] Those attacks came upon him because Las Casas did not only exercise Christian charity towards the indigenous population but constructed a theologically informed defence of their human rights because of their condition as children of God made in his own image.[49]

In his defence of the indigenous populations, Las Casas resembled Job, another biblical figure important for Gutiérrez. If Gutiérrez dwells on the suffering of the innocent by examining the book of Job he does so by associating the person of Job not with a passive sufferer but with an example of suffering-trust in God and his love for all.[50] Job in the Bible and Bartolomé de las Casas in the Latin American context become prototypes of Christian history because they are able not only to empathize with those suffering but because, in enduring physical and emotional suffering themselves, they see God not through a general depersonalized historical narrative but with the poor as protagonists of that history. Thus, they develop a theology that speaks once and again of the love of God in a human history in need of liberation and not in a theology ridden with clauses, argumentations and intellectual discourses attached to the learned and to the philosophers. In the case of Las Casas:

> Bartolomé welds faith to what we today would call social analysis. This enables him to unmask the 'social sin' of his time. That, doubtless, was his forte – and also the difference

between him and the great majority of those in Spain who were concerned with the affairs of the Indies ... Those who had not seen the abuse and contempt to which the Indians were subjected, those who had not suffered in their own flesh the aggression of the mighty ones of the Indies, those who had not counted dead bodies, had other priorities in theology.[51]

In that period between 1968 and 1994 the ongoing changes in the world, with the end of the Cold War and the diminishing authority of the Church in Europe, triggered a shift between theology understood as European systematic theology to theologies that were triggered within the majority churches outside Europe. Such theology became a response to a plausible divine presence within underdevelopment, poverty, inhumanity, human rights violations, the genocide of indigenous populations and the destruction of the planet. The same experience of death by poverty and underdevelopment was the experience of a parish priest, Gustavo Gutiérrez, at the beginning of his journey in 1968. In Chimbote, Peru, addressing priests, he developed the seeds of a theology of liberation not speaking about revolution and liberation by armed struggle but of the liberation of a God who was and is articulated walking with the poor. The 'power of the poor' was the power of the realization that God was walking with them not as a master or as a landowner but as the God of life who preferred to walk with the humble and those who, being materially poor, were rich in the spirit of the Sermon on the Mount. Others found resonance in Gutiérrez' theology because that was the context of poverty not only in the Latin America of the 1970s and 1980s but also in the slums of Africa and the challenges of colonialism, as well as the oppression of outcastes in India and non-Buddhists in other Asian countries. The theology of liberation discovered not only a theological method in which theology was a second step but developed a hermeneutics of suspicion and the great joy and celebration of a God who loved humanity in the poor and at the same time not only helped to liberate them from poverty and oppression but was defined as a Liberator.

Liberation Theology after Rwanda

But as theologians of the third world were progressing in their deliberations and were becoming established throughout the European and North American publishing houses, death became apparent once again. The international community and the Church had to witness the massive killings triggered by extremists in Rwanda, but bound together with a past experience of a triumphant and colonial Church. The Rwanda genocide marked a new period of theology, in which God seemed to have been silent when Hutu extremists and their elitist ideology of racism managed to exterminate close to 1 million Tutsi and Hutu moderates. The beautiful and rising theology of inculturation and the local theologies of many Africans seemed crushed in a period in which theology became divided between theology before and after the Rwanda genocide. And after Rwanda came ethnic cleansing in the former Yugoslavia; this time theology had to encounter the resurgence of a sick nationalism in which Christian history, monasteries and faith were used as a justification for the elimination of Muslims. Such insensitivity was difficult to witness even within the European Union, and long after the end of the Second World War. Death had arrived at Srebrenica, and the theology of genocide and ethnic cleansing was not what was intended after the time of military regimes in Latin America, Africa and Asia and the collapse of a divided world symbolized by the Berlin Wall. Darfur and East Timor and the wars in the Middle East dominated this second period of liberation theology and the theology of the poor because God was present through the churches and people, even when death, hunger and poverty were also present. For, I argued during that period, God was even there in a torture chamber being tortured with electricity, water boards, and animals in the prisoners' vaginas.[52] I was present in Latin America and Africa when inhumanity tried to silence God and God was not silent. Through human hands, solidarity and hope, God walked with her people and was punished together with them.

Yes, this present theological thinking returns to the experiences of the theology of suffering and of the poor of Latin

America that I had experienced in those years of military violence against opponents and against my own body, the cholera epidemics and malaria fits of eastern Africa, the wars between brothers in Somalia, and the Rwanda genocide almost thirty years ago. I searched for the possibility of reflection in St Andrews for 26 years, and suddenly and unexpectedly I found myself in Chile attending a conference a few days before the Chilean quarantine, and the closing of the frontiers and the absence of planes from Europe left me behind and with the poor of Santiago. Terror invaded me many times during this time because I had become accustomed to the securities of Europe. My trips to India in order to visit and to dialogue with Hindus and Buddhists were marked by the protection I was given by colleagues and friends.

However, in March 2020 I was left on my own in a flat in downtown Santiago surrounded by immigrants, older people without families, and youth with many plans but little security for the future. And with three budgies as companions, I started a very long period of isolation marked by small shopping trips undertaken in two family shops that reminded me of my younger years in a Santiago shanty town or the dusty towns of the Arab trade routes in Africa. I was one of the privileged ones, with a place of my own, a classical music station on, the occasional call from my doctoral students in Scotland, and the ongoing presence of the British media who wanted my advice on solitude, prayer and life as a hermit. I spoke several times to the BBC on prayer and fear, on the guidance of Pope Francis and the Dalai Lama. I spoke of the kindness and warmth of the humble and the poor, who took special care of me, an older and foreign man, when I was searching for apples or for ham in order to have a treat. Those foods, off limits to those who earn between 300 and 400 dollars a month and who manage to feed their families, sometimes of six to eight people, reminded me of how I had managed to compromise the journey shown to me by Pedro Casaldáliga and many others. And I asked myself, what kind of God is speaking to us among the poor and within the pandemic? What kind of message is God giving us? What would be the lessons learned from this period for the time after isolation? And I started writing about the third period of the theologies of the poor, very much as in the first period, with the poor and the marginalized of Santiago. Isolation for the poor was a curse because they needed to find something to sell in order to live as industry, construction and schooling came to a halt. Most of the dead came from poor neighbourhoods as families could not isolate themselves within their own homes and as hunger spread through neighbourhoods. Hunger, fear, and sickness spread through the streets nearby, and my profession or many academic titles did not matter: I was an older man to be kept safe, and neighbours started offering help with rubbish and shopping as I was on my own, and as my appearance became that of anybody of my age in the neighbourhood, with unkempt hair, with no washing machine, and with the fear of dying in the pandemic without a name, a past, my life companion or my friends and colleagues.

The God of the pandemic has been a very close and warm God; however, it has been a long time since I did walk with a God who reminded me that through sickness and the coronavirus we could die sooner than we expected, and that no learned book we had written could prevent such a moment. God is in control, not us, and he is the one who made this period possible. But God manifests his life through the context and through the poor and the marginalized. As Gutiérrez has stated, theology is a 'second act', praxis is first. Thus, my sense of tranquillity when, on 3 June, a message came from the administrator of the building I lived in telling residents that one of the night watchmen had been diagnosed with the virus and that one resident with a family had also been diagnosed and that the person had not informed anybody for a week. My thoughts and my heart turned to God on that night and to the many who were hungry around me under the winter rain and the temperature of 4°C after that day's rain.

This work is a theological reflection from the praxis of being with the poor in the pandemic, and the experience of the common food pots, and the hungry poor who come first because they show us the presence of God first, while this theological reflection comes second, out of such experience.

It reminds me that I spoke to Brazilian students about my theological work online and I only wanted to tell them not to miss God in the poor during the pandemic. For the radicality of the gospel taught us once more during the pandemic that Jesus walked with us again on our streets, and we will never be the same. God walked on the streets of Santiago, and I want to reflect with you on that walk because it was as if I was on the *Titanic* and had been left in a third-class cabin among sickness, death and poverty; but there I saw happiness and solidarity – and God walked among his people once again. For a couple of weeks there were no boats to leave the scene, and no mechanical ventilators, and God, the budgies and I listened to Mahler's Resurrection Symphony, cosily waiting, because God was walking Lord Cochrane Street during the pandemic.

In this book I will reflect on the liberating praxis of action, human and divine action, and I will expand on an interreligious pandemic that has enlarged the plausibility of a theology after Rwanda and after Somalia. For theological reflections after sharing food and wine with the poor and the marginalized have been a common phenomenon of the Kingdom in Santiago, Kolkata, Dharamshala, Hargeisa and Kigali throughout this pandemic and we have shared such experiences online. Through the wonders of international communications, we learned how to communicate with human beings who through being alone were closer to God, and we learned how human beings with the coronavirus became lepers, outcasts and a danger to the powerful, as had been the case in the time of Jesus. The lessons of such experience were summarized by the Dalai Lama and Pope Francis on gathering many in order to empower them with the experience of something beyond consumerism and prosperity: indeed, to entrust them with a new world and a new cosmos, Maranatha!

In this period after the 'first wave' of the pandemic it is not possible to wait for the end of the pandemic. We have been told ad nauseam that there is no such end, but that we must change, we must experience social change that leads to less sociability, to an inward sense of our family and safety, to fewer signs of care for others such as kisses, handshakes and public moments of togetherness. A new rethinking of our life, our experience of God and our liberation from sin, poverty and oppression must also take place. In the field of liberation theology we already had a vacuum, not only because there were fewer publications in such a field, but because the latest gurus either exited the centrality of the northern hemisphere and its brilliant lights or they sent one of its brightest pastors and spiritual leaders – Jorge Mario Bergoglio, currently known as Pope Francis – to the northern hemisphere, even when technically he is in the southern tip of Europe. However, the theologies of the poor re-localized themselves to the majority churches with the result that within publishing houses they became less prominent. For example, the challenges of cooperation between Latin American and Latino theologians arose out of a context in which, at the beginning of the twenty-first century, theologians of liberation relocated their discourse to the American Academy of Religion to the detriment of the peripheries. However, before the death of Marcella Althaus-Reid and the relocation of Ivan Petrella to Argentina, the subject of the poor and the marginalized was focused on economics and gender through a common project triggered by Petrella on rethinking liberation theology vis-à-vis economics and the work of Mo-Sung. Within such theology there was a self-critique to liberation theology on two fronts: a critique of the lack of engagement with economics and globalization (Petrella), and the failure to address gender and transgender issues (Althaus-Reid).

On the other side of the global critique, Asian and African theologians were engaged in a critique of the end of empire and of the oppression of minorities through caste, majority religions and Islamic fundamentalism. Within all these critiques the challenge was to foster a universal understanding of contextual liberation theology versus European theology. In my work on the Rwanda genocide I criticized the over-engagement of liberation theology and interfaith theologies with an academic acceptance that ended with the unintended exit of Petrella and the death of Althaus-Reid.[53] The end of such an era was marked by Christian–Hindu dialogue and the declaration of the shared humanity in St Andrews (September 2016), and the relocation of theologies of context towards resistance, such as those of Dalit theologians, a challenge to caste in India, and the possibilities of contextual hybridity by African theologians such as Agbonkhianmeghe Orobator, Musa Dube and Mercy Oduyoye.[54] It is at these crossroads after pandemics that a theology of death brings a fresh reflection on the centrality of the poor and the marginalized by applying an orthopraxis to the periphery of the world once again. For the inequality of the poor and the marginalized, at the margins and within the majority churches outside the West brings a renewed agenda of what Juan Luis Segundo called 'the lost and recovered history of Jesus of Nazareth'.[55] For that history is as contextual today as it was yesterday, and such recovery must include the dialogue and journey with other religions, not only in Asia or Africa but also in Latin America. Thus, *Querida Amazonia* or *Laudato Si'* have arrived as documents of dialogue, of a journey of learning that have been politically and theologically influenced by the *imago Dei* as the God of humanity, the God of the poor and the one that leads a humanizing process in Pedro Trigo's sharp diachronic analysis.[56] Within the image of God and the voices of God in all religions, I have taken the pandemic as a period of learning from more than fifty female theologians, never cited in the literature, and introduce some of the Asian female theologians within this work.

In Chapter 1, I explore the cries of the poor in different countries such as India, Chile and Somaliland, and the response of solidarity and humanity that has gone beyond fear and anxiety. The poor have a clear sense that God is not punishing them but that God is again being allowed to walk with us – the crying praxis of Emmaus and the solitude of emptiness replaces and challenges the atonement and the intellectualization of the incarnation. People of all religions find a purpose in helping the needy, and cease to feel that they are enemies, as temples, churches and mosques are closed for fear of the pandemic, and their solidarity arises out of different and contested beliefs. God becomes public in the home sphere once again rather than in the mega temples of noise and power.

In the Chapter 2, I explore issues of migration and how

the closing of borders for Indian migrants, returning Europeans and workers during the pandemic resembled an initial
chaos and public fear. It is an experiential and biographical
chapter of an experience of border closing that occurred with
the announcement of the Partition of India, or when Jesus and
his parents visited the Temple in Jerusalem. For, situations of
lockdown and isolation divide once again the well-to-do, who
have transport, home space and resources, and the poor who
continue moving in order to eat, knowing that to do otherwise would mean hunger and annihilation. However, this time
I was left behind without a plane, and I started learning from
the poor how to survive, how to find God and how to react
to human solidarity, hunger and pestilence. As described by
Paulo Freire, the pedagogy of the oppressed became my new
schooling, as it was in the past when I was tortured and when
several times I had to learn from other faiths and other truths.
My diary of pandemic days is a diary in which I hang on to my
life as the fear of being infected became an experience of tranquillity with the poor and the immigrants of Santiago, who are
used to having their freedom and their desire limited by their
lack of economic means and opportunities within society.

Chapter 3 explores some of the masters of a shared humanity
who have managed to inspire this post-pandemic theology: for
example, Pope Francis (*Laudato Si'*, *Querida Amazonia*), the
Dalai Lama (Universal Responsibility), Mohammad Khatami
of Iran (against the clash of civilizations), the Jesuit A. E.
Orobator (Christianity, Islam, indigenous religions in Africa),
Mariano Puga (Chile), Felipe Berríos SJ (Chile), José Aldunate
SJ (Chile), Eve Parker (UK/India), James Morris (UK/Japan),
Pedro Trigo SJ (Venezuela). It is here that the reflection of the
encounter of different faiths becomes part of that dangerous
water in which theologizing becomes not a safe profession
but a dangerous proposition. We have gone to the dangerous
streets of encounter with the Other where the Divine lives, and
we feel the danger of such theologizing, for we are not safe
any longer. This is not the world of theological faculties or
majestic libraries, but it is here in the *terra incognita* that God
lives beyond the market and beyond the state.[57] The market

has crashed, and is facing difficulties; the market is dead as a principle of global unity, long live the market!

Chapter 4 explores the common purpose of dialogue in the past years and during the pandemic. It looks at the cooperation between the different faith communities to help neighbour and others, again with an emphasis on India, South America and Africa. It argues that it is through praxis that good will between faith communities starts returning to the basics of each world religion based on the respect for life, the presence of the Divine in the world, and the compassion and solidarity that many times has been forgotten. After the pandemic these theologies can operate in a common purpose of learning from the poor and finding a divine presence in the world of those who fear and are oppressed. Interfaith dialogue as praxis becomes the foundation for a shared humanity in which the divinity is present and not the other way around. Once we become poor, as God is, we move without return to find God with complete commitment to liberate all from injustice because God lives with and in the poor and the marginalized.

Chapter 5 explores and describes the characteristic of a post-pandemic theology associated with a liberating praxis. It is the experience of a shared fear of the virus, the pandemic, that allows us to be aware once again of a shared belonging, of our universal responsibility and of a shared planet. Within such experience and the theological reflection that follows, we experience the multiple belonging in the diversity in that realm that Archbishop Tutu called 'the God of the rainbow'. Multiple belonging becomes the essence of existence in a post-pandemic theology. We belong to many because God is the infinite diversity that humans cannot comprehend, and the liberation of theology as described by J. L. Segundo becomes the liberation of God from our chains and our theological prejudices. It is the freedom of the marginalized that makes theology secondary and insignificant to the orthopraxis of the divine liturgy of the cosmos. Poetry unites such diversity through the language of God in Ernesto Cardenal, Teilhard de Chardin, Pedro Casaldáliga and Raimon Panikkar. The liberating God is discovered in the music of those who suffer hunger and discrimination today, and it is a concert of the senses, a divine music. After pestilence it is in the world of the divine incarnation where God walks once again as we see the presence of the dead and the infirm because God is among them.

Notes

1 Pope Francis, 'Extraordinary Moment of Prayer Presided Over by Pope Francis', Sagrato of St Peter's Basilica, Friday 27 March 2020, Vatican City: Libreria Editrice Vaticana.

2 'Pope faces coronavirus "tempest" alone in St. Peter's Square', *The Bangkok Post*, 28 March 2020, at www.bangkokpost.com/world/1888180/pope-faces-coronavirus-tempest-alone-in-st-peters-square, accessed 31.8.20.

3 I have dwelt on these issues of contested epistemologies at the core of this postcolonial distinction elsewhere, with particular reference to the colonial language of Hegel in the original German text. See Mario I. Aguilar, 'Postcolonial African Theology in Kabasele Lumbala', *Theological Studies* 63/2 (2002), pp. 302–23.

4 The case of the Spanish Flu has been used as a comparative in history. It lasted from the European spring of 1918 to early summer 1919. It infected about 500 million people, a third of the world's population at that time. See Laura Spinney, *Pale Rider: The Spanish Flu of 1918 and How It Changed the World*, London: Vintage, 2018; and Mark Honigsbaum, *The Pandemic Century: One Hundred Years of Panic, Hysteria, and Hubris*, London: W. W. Norton & Company, 2019.

5 Joseph Cardinal Ratzinger, *God is Near Us: The Eucharist, the Heart of Life*, San Francisco, CA: Ignatius Press, 2006.

6 William T. Cavanaugh, *Torture and Eucharist: Theology, Politics and the Body of Christ*, Oxford: Blackwell, 1998; and Damian Onwuegbuchulam, *The Eucharist as Orikonso: A Study in Eucharist Ecclesiology from an Igbo Perspective*, Bern: Peter Lang, 2008.

7 Roberto Morozzo Della Rocca, *Oscar Romero: Prophet of Hope*, London: Darton Longman & Todd, 2015.

8 Rodolfo Cardenal, *Historia de una esperanza: Vida de Rutilio Grande*, San Salvador: UCA, 1985; and Teresa Whitfield, *Paying the Price: Ignacio Ellacuria and the Murdered Jesuits of El Salvador*, Philadelphia, PA: Temple University Press, 1994.

9 Robert Lassalle-Klein, *Blood and Ink: Ignacio Ellacuría, Jon Sobrino and the Jesuit Martyrs of the University of Central America*, Maryknoll, NY: Orbis, 2014.

10 Stephen Bevans and Katalina Tahaafe-Williams (eds), *Contextual Theology for the Twenty-First Century*, Eugene, OR: Pickwick Publications, 2011; Paul S. Chung, Veli Matti Karkkainen and Kim Kyoung-Jae (eds), *Asian Contextual Theology for the Third Millennium*, Eugene, OR: Pickwick Publications, 2007; and Flora A. Keshgegian, *Redeeming Memories: A Theology of Healing and Transformation*, Nashville, TN: Abingdon Press, 2000.

11 Erik Peterson, *Theological Tractates*, Palo Alto, CA: Stanford University Press, 2011. I would argue that such critique has been answered and moved forward through the pioneering work of Francesca Stavrakopoulou, *Land of Our Fathers: The Roles of Ancestor Veneration in Biblical Land Claims*, London: T&T Clark, 2010.

12 Elizabeth Phillips, *Political Theology: A Guide for the Perplexed*, London: T&T Clark International, 2012.

13 It could be argued that the zikkaron (memorial, act of memory) is already contextual as it was during Christ's supper in Jerusalem. I acknowledge the guidance of Fr Ottone Cantore on these issues during my studies of memory in Israel in 1986 for my Master's thesis on B. S. Child. Indeed, memory and the memory of the people of God has become central to the developments of liberation theology; see Mary Grey, 'Liberation Theology and the Bearers of Dangerous Memory', *New Blackfriars* 75/887, pp. 512–24.

14 Johann Baptist Metz, *Faith in History and Society: Towards a Practical Fundamental Theology*, New York: Seabury, 1980.

15 Johann Baptist Metz, *Theology of the World*, New York: Seabury, 1969.

16 Johann Baptist Metz, *A Passion for God: The Mystical-Political Dimension of Christianity*, New York: Paulist Press, 1997.

17 Gustavo Gutiérrez, *A Theology of Liberation: History, Politics, and Salvation*, 15th anniversary edn with new Introduction by the author, Maryknoll, NY: Orbis, 1988; and Lilian Calles Barger, *The World Come of Age: An Intellectual History of Liberation Theology*, New York: Oxford University Press, 2018.

18 See for example, Susan L. Burns, *Kingdom of the Sick: A History of Leprosy and Japan*, Honolulu, Hawaii: University of Hawaii Press, 2019.

19 Pierre Sourisseau, *Charles de Foucauld 1858–1916: Biographie*, Paris: Salvator, 2016.

20 *Gaudium et Spes* § 1.

21 Mario I. Aguilar, '1968: A Historiography of a New Reformation in Latin America', *Schweizerische Zeitschrift für Religions- und Kulturgeschichte* 104 (2010), pp. 201–11.

22 For an overview of Vatican II's impact on Latin America, see Enrique Dussel, 'Latin America', in Adrian Hastings (ed), *Modern Catholicism: Vatican II and After*, London: SPCK, and New York:

Oxford University Press, 1991, pp. 319–25; see also Enrique Dussel, *Historia de la Iglesia en América Latina: Coloniaje y Liberación (1492–1983)*, Madrid: Esquela Misional, 1983; and *Los últimos 50 años (1930–1985) en la historia de la Iglesia en América Latina*, Bogotá: Indo American Press, 1986.

23 Among the many works that cover the genesis and development of the CEBs, see Leonardo Boff, *Eclesiogênese: As comunidades eclesiais de base reinventam a Igreja*, Petrópolis: Editora Vozes, 1977, and 'Comunidades eclesiais de base: povo oprimido que se organiza para a libertaçao', *Revista Eclesiástica Brasileira* 41 (June 1981), pp. 312–30. English translation of both Portuguese works published as Leonardo Boff, *Ecclesiogenesis: The Base Communities Reinvent the Church*, Maryknoll, NY: Orbis, 1986; Thomas C. Bruneau, *The Political Transformation of the Brazilian Catholic Church*, New York: Cambridge University Press, 1974; and *The Church in Brazil*, Austin: University of Texas Press, 1982; W. E. Hewitt, *Base Christian Communities and Social Change in Brazil*, Lincoln and London: University of Nebraska Press, 1991; Cardinal Aloísio Lorscheider, 'Fifty Years of the CNBB: A Bishop's Conference Based on the Council – Evangelization Projects, Political and Ecclesiastical Tensions and Challenges', in José Oscar Beozzo and Luiz Carlos Susin (eds), *Brazil: People and Church(es)* (*Concilium* 2002), pp. 25–30; Scott Mainwaring, *The Catholic Church and Politics in Brazil 1916–1985*, Stanford: Stanford University Press, 1986; Maria Helena Moreira Alves, *Estado e oposição no Brasil 1964–1984*, Petrópolis: Editora Vozes, 1984.

24 For an overview of these ten years, see Enrique Dussel, *De Medellín a Puebla: una década de sangre y esperanza (1968–1979)*, Mexico City: CEE-Edicol.

25 This ecclesial renewal of Latin America also affected the Reformed churches in Latin America. See Guillermo Cook, *The Expectation of the Poor: Latin American Basic Ecclesial Communities in Protestant Perspectives*, Maryknoll, NY: Orbis, 1985; see also Mario I. Aguilar, 'The Kairos of Medellin: Towards a Movement for Liberation and New Mission after Vatican II', in Patrick Claffey and Joe Egan (eds), *Movement or Moment: Assessing Liberation Theology Forty Years after Medellín*, Bern: Peter Lang, 2009, pp. 9–28; and '1968: A Historiography of a New Reformation in Latin America', *Schweizerische Zeitschrift für Religions- und Kulturgeschichte* 104 (2010), pp. 201–11.

26 Leonardo Boff, 'A Theological Examination of the Terms "People of God" and "Popular Church"', in Leonardo Boff and Virgil Elizondo (eds), *La Iglesia Popular: Between Fear and Hope* (*Concilium* 176, 1984/6), pp. 89–97.

27 Mario I. Aguilar, *Theology, Liberation and Genocide: A Theology of the Periphery*, London: SCM Press, 2009.

28 Aguilar, *Theology, Liberation and Genocide*, p. 69.

29 Gustavo Gutiérrez, 'Theological Language: Fullness of Silence', in Gustavo Gutiérrez, *The Density of the Present: Selected Writings*, Maryknoll, NY: Orbis, 1999, p. 186, from 'Address on the occasion of his induction to the Peruvian Academy of Spanish Language 1995', full original in *Páginas* 137 (1996), pp. 66–87.

30 Gustavo Gutiérrez, 'Mirar lejos: Introducción a la decimocuarta edición', in *Teología de la liberación: Perspectivas*, Salamanca: Ediciones Sígueme, 16th edn, 1999 (Lima: Centro de Estudios y Publicaciones 1971), p. 38.

31 Theology as a poetic narrative on God's presence and action in the world presupposes a changing paradigm, thus it is no longer possible to write about Gutiérrez' theological work by just focusing on his major initial work *Teología de la liberación*.

32 The theological periods within the original Spanish texts are clearly chronological and they follow theological reflections that arise out of preparations for the meeting of Latin American Bishops at Medellin, Puebla and Santo Domingo. These periods are more difficult to isolate within the published works in English due to the fact that Gutiérrez has not published everything he has ever written and not everything published in other languages has been translated into the English language. Frei Betto has suggested, 'It is quite likely that he is the author of more unpublished texts, known only to a small circle of readers, than of published works. Usually he does not even sign the mimeographed texts, which include an excellent introduction to the ideas of Marx and Engels and their relationship to Christianity': Frei Betto, 'Gustavo Gutiérrez – A Friendly Profile', in Marc H. Ellis and Otto Maduro (eds), *The Future of Liberation Theology: Essays in Honor of Gustavo Gutiérrez*, Maryknoll, NY: Orbis, 1989, pp. 31–7, at p. 35.

33 Gutiérrez has been criticized for having been influenced by modernity and its romantic idealism; however, it is clear that the thought of Gutiérrez in the 1960s and 1970s was influenced by the Latin American context in which the Pauline vision of the 'new man' was also used by socialist discourses associated with the Cuban revolution and with a socialist conception of revolution led by the icon of Ché Guevara; see Mariano Delgado, '"Esperanza plañe entre algodones": Cuando Gustavo Gutiérrez habla de dios', in *Teología de la liberación: Cruce de miradas*, Coloquio de Friburgo, April 1999, Lima: Instituto Bartolomé de Las Casas-Rímac and Centro de Estudios y Publicaciones, 2000, pp. 101–32, at pp. 102–3; cf. Michael Sievernich, 'Von der Utopie zur Ethik. Zur Theologie von Gustavo Gutiérrez', *Theologie und Philosophie* 71 (1996), pp. 33–46.

34 Gutiérrez gave the name to an ecclesial reflection that had already taken place, thus 'liberation theology is not a new growth of Christian theological reflection, but rather an outgrowth of long years of such

reflection', William Boteler MM, 'Greetings', in Ellis and Maduro (eds), *The Future of Liberation Theology*, pp. 13–15, at p. 13.

35 It is clear that 'the influence of Gustavo [Gutiérrez] on theological method and praxis began in Peru long before the concretization of that influence took place in books and at high-level church conferences. Taking time to work with groups of persons – delegates of the word, pastoral agents, local religious, student groups, missionaries – became the modus operandi of these young Peruvian priests'; see Luise Ahrens MM and Barbara Hendricks MM, in Ellis and Maduro (eds), *The Future of Liberation Theology*, pp. 3–4.

36 Langdon Gilkey, 'The Political Dimensions of Theology', in Brian Mahan and L. Dale Richesin (eds), *The Challenge of Liberation Theology: A First World Response*, Maryknoll, NY: Orbis, 1981, p. 117; Inaugural Lecture as the Shailer Mathews Professor in the Divinity School of the University of Chicago, pp. 113–26.

37 Chimbote is described as 'a coastal fishing port to the north of Lima noted for his [*sic*] astounding stench and pollution produced by local fishmeal factories and steel mills. A small version of Lima, Chimbote harbors masses of exploited, impoverished workers who have come from the Peruvian sierra in search of work, only to find themselves unemployed and living in hellish, concentric circles of mat houses that surround the city'; see Curt Cadorette, 'Peru and the Mystery of Liberation: The Nexus and Logic of Gustavo Gutiérrez' Theology', in Ellis and Maduro (eds), *The Future of Liberation Theology*, pp. 49–58, at p. 53.

38 Gutiérrez, *A Theology of Liberation* is dedicated to Arguedas, Gutiérrez' close friend and fellow writer, both influenced by Peru's socialist thinker José Carlos Mariátegui (1895–1930), and to the Brazilian priest Henrique Pereira Neto, assassinated in Recife on 26 May 1969; see Betto, 'Gustavo Gutiérrez – A Friendly Profile', in Ellis and Maduro (eds), *The Future of Liberation Theology*, pp. 31–7, 32, 37; and Stephen Judd MM, 'Gustavo Gutiérrez and the Originality of the Peruvian experience', in Ellis and Maduro (eds), *The Future of Liberation Theology*, pp. 65–76, at pp. 66–7.

39 Since 2001, Gutiérrez has held the John Cardinal O'Hara Chair in Theology at the University of Notre Dame. Otherwise he lived in Rimac, 'a gray, dirty, noisy slum where residents are frantically trying to survive, to find or keep a job, to feed and clothe their children. It is a place where struggle is a common denominator and hope, however tenuous, is a thin thread that holds human lives together': Curt Cadorette, 'Peru and the Mystery of Liberation', in Ellis and Maduro (eds), *The Future of Liberation Theology*, 1989, pp. 49–58, at p. 49.

40 Gustavo Gutiérrez, *La fuerza histórica de los pobres*, Lima: Centro de Estudios y Publicaciones, 1979, English translation, *The Power of the Poor in History*, Maryknoll, NY: Orbis, 1983.

41 *Gaudium et Spes* § 45.

42 Gustavo Gutiérrez, 'Toward a Theology of Liberation', in James B. Nickoloff (ed.), *Gustavo Gutiérrez: Essential Writings*, London: SCM Press, 1996, p. 27.

43 Juan Alfaro, 'God Protects and Liberates the Poor – O.T.', *Concilium* 187 (1986), pp. 27–35; Leonardo Boff and Virgil Elizondo (eds), *Option for the Poor: Challenge to the Rich Countries*, Edinburgh: T&T Clark, 1986.

44 Gustavo Gutiérrez, 'God's Revelation and Proclamation in History', in *The Power of the Poor in History: Selected Writings*, London: SCM Press, 1983, p. 6.

45 Gutiérrez prefers the term 'encounter' or 'collision', while those reading history from a European viewpoint term it 'discovery' or 'conquest' and others even term it 'invasion' or 'covering'; Gustavo Gutiérrez, *Las Casas: In Search of the Poor of Jesus Christ*, Maryknoll, NY: Orbis, 1993, p. 2.

46 It was in that context that the Jesuits developed safe places around the borders of current Argentina, Paraguay and Brazil, for indigenous peoples to live in well-bounded territories where they learned about Christianity, worked on the land, lived communally and escaped the enslaving mechanisms of the Portuguese slavers. The Jesuits were expelled from the Portuguese colonies in 1759, from France in 1762, and from the Spanish colonies in 1767. On 21 July 1773, Pope Clement XIV suspended the mere existence of the Society of Jesus: Michel Clévenot, 'The Kingdom of God on Earth? The Jesuit Reductions of Paraguay', *Concilium* 187 (1986), pp. 70–7; Leonardo Boff and Virgil Elizondo (eds), *Option for the Poor: Challenge to the Rich Countries*, Edinburgh: T&T Clark, 1986.

47 Gustavo Gutiérrez, *En busca de los pobres de Jesucristo*, Lima: Instituto Bartolomé de las Casas-Rimac and Centro de Estudios y Publicaciones, 1992.

48 However, Las Casas was not, according to Gutiérrez, an isolated prophetic voice but he was part of a minority group that included missionaries, bishops, civil servants and even members of the royal court who expressed their concern about the fate of the Indians under the conquistadors: Gutiérrez, *Las Casas*, p. 5.

49 Lewis Hanke, *Aristotle and the American Indians: A Study in Race Prejudice in the Modern World*, London: Hollis & Carter, Chicago: Henry Regnery, 1959; *All the Peoples of the World are Men: The Disputation between Bartolomé de Las Casas and Juan Ginés de Sepúlveda in 1550 on the Intellectual and Religious Capacity of the American Indians*, Minneapolis: University of Minnesota Press, 1970; *All Mankind is One: A Study of the Disputation between Bartolomé de Las Casas and Juan Ginés de Sepúlveda in 1550 on the Intellectual and Religious Capacity of the American Indians*, Dekalb: Northern Illinois University Press, 1974.

50 Gustavo Gutiérrez, *On Job: God-Talk and the Suffering of the Innocent*, Maryknoll, NY: Orbis, 1987.

51 Gutiérrez, *Las Casas*, pp. 6–7. Gutiérrez refers to Las Casas' account of the atrocities done by the conquistadors: *A Short Account of the Destruction of the Indies*, London: Penguin, with chronology and further reading 2004 [1992].

52 Mario I. Aguilar, *Religion, Torture and the Liberation of God*, New York: Routledge, 2015.

53 Mario I. Aguilar, *Theology, Liberation, Genocide: A Theology of the Periphery*, London: SCM Press, 2009.

54 Mario I. Aguilar, *Christian Ashrams, Hindu Caves, and Sacred Rivers: Christian–Hindu Monastic Dialogue in India 1950–1993*, London and Philadelphia: Jessica Kingsley, 2016; *The Way of the Hermit: Interfaith Encounters in Silence and Prayer*, London and Philadelphia: Jessica Kingsley, 2017; and *Interreligious Dialogue and the Partition of India: Hindus and Muslims in Dialogue about Violence and Forced Migration*, London and Philadelphia: Jessica Kingsley, 2018.

55 Juan Luis Segundo SJ, *Historia perdida y recuperada de Jesús de Nazaret*, Santander: Sal Terrae, 1991.

56 Pedro Trigo Durá SJ, *Dios y Padre de nuestro Señor Jesucristo: En el cristianismo latinoamericano*, Santander: Sal Terrae, 2020.

57 On beyond the market, see Pedro Trigo SJ, *En el mercado de Dios, Un Dios más allá del mercado*. Santander: Sal Tarrae, 2003.

1

A Crying Praxis of a Shared Humanity

The pandemic of 2020 brought a new challenge to the divisions of globalization and the ills of capitalism: that of a pandemic and post-pandemic in which money and financial networks could not save one's life or those of one's family because of infection and food shortage.[1] One could argue that if in the 1990s the death of the state was declared, during the pandemic financial markets were not able to save themselves and the importance of solidarity and states' policies of social aid and solidarity compensated for the inability of financial markets to sustain peace and health. Economic indicators and financial international models needed to be sharply re-evaluated because quarantines in Europe and elsewhere meant a stop in commercial activities, including transportation of passengers and tourism.[2]

Those who couldn't work because of quarantine suffered the financial consequences, and in countries where the state didn't take care of the poor and marginalized there was hunger, sickness and pestilence.[3] For example, despite positive economic indicators in Chile before the pandemic, priests who lived with the poor and lived by their work, such as the Jesuit Felipe Berríos, became catalysts of solidarity and critics of a state that also tried to save the rich. Forty years ago, another worker priest, the Jesuit José (Pepe) Aldunate, had written about hunger in Chile and the community pots that sustained so many families and children.[4] Aldunate, a priest who had been at the forefront of a movement against torture in Chile during the period of the military, wrote often about hunger

not as a condition of personal want but as a permanent condition that impeded the biological development of human
beings, especially children who during classes fainted because
they had not had breakfast. The images of Chilean television
were clear: while in the rich suburbs of Santiago the quarantine seemed to be a stop, an interruption in between periods
of life, for others on the poorer side of the city, who didn't
have a heated home during winter, the only solution was to
depend on the generosity of neighbours, parishes and NGOs.
Common pots (*ollas comunes*), where hundreds of people
could be fed at least one meal a day, were organized. It was
no different from 40 years ago, and once again the Catholic
Church and the Jesuits, through their service to refugees, the
elderly and those without families, were at the forefront of
such gospel-oriented help.[5]

On 20 March 2020, Pope Francis asked the Dicastery for
Promoting Integral Human Development (DPIHD) to create
a Commission to express solicitude and care for the whole
human family facing Covid-19, including an ongoing analysis
and a reflection on the new socio-economic-cultural future.[6]
The Commission, through five working groups, outlined the
sense of immediacy and emergency that was immediately understood by Pope Francis and that was confirmed by accounts
of poverty and hunger outlined by seminal reflections such as
Gaudium et Spes, Populorum Progressio, and *Laudato Si'*.[7] The
working groups were organized under the following headings:
'acting now for the future', 'looking to the future with creativity', 'communicating hope', 'seeking common dialogue and
reflections' and 'supporting to care'. They included a security
task force, an economic task force, an ecology task force and
a health task force.[8] The task forces provided a response to
requests that came to the Vatican and to Pope Francis from
all quarters of the world, and the economics task force drove
a campaign for inclusive changes in economic policy by all
countries but especially the rich countries and the European
Union.[9] Mechanical ventilators and different contributions to
the homeless, the elderly and immigrants were sent from the
Vatican throughout the pandemic, in a manner that was to

set Pope Francis' ongoing involvement with gospel ideas in a financial world of inequality that was collapsing.

Pope Francis, in his daily speeches, emphasized the involvement of the Church (1.3 billion people all over the world) in fulfilling the spirit of the gospel in Matthew 25, concerning the service of neighbour in the name of Christ. 'For I was hungry, and you gave me to eat, and I was in prison and you visited me, I was naked and you clothed me.' The pandemic brought a liberating revival and a return to the theological practices of a post-Vatican II Church and the modus operandi of the first generation of liberation theologians. As was done through universities and pastoral centres previously, communities fostered information from social scientists in order to pressurize social and political change in the name of the gospel. It is here that I advance some theological reflections that I will expand upon in the last chapter of this book: the diversity of liberation theologies in Catholic, Reformed and post-Christian worlds came together in interfaith dialogue responses.[10] They showed that different faith communities can walk together the same journey within the diversity and multiplicity of their traditions. Thus, ways of serving Christ in the poor and the marginalized could be varied but sustained and lived in unity. Multiple belonging in One but through many remains the post-pandemic way of actualizing Pentecost within the churches, and of the churches in the contemporary world. Thus, Patriarch Bartholomew, the Dalai Lama, the Archbishop of Canterbury and the World Council of Churches spoke the same message of solidarity in the name of the gospel. However, the Christian challenge was not only to provide aid to the needy, the sick and the elderly but it carried a harsh critique to the financial systems and global companies that had enriched themselves while those who lost their jobs were left without bread for their families.

Within such a global scenario I return to a central criticism and prophetic understanding by an older generation of liberation theologians: the neo-liberal model of a market economy has not benefited the grounding of gospel values. Instead, it has strengthened personal individualism, competition and selfishness rather than the cooperation and solidarity in which the

poor have the same rights as those who are better off finan-
cially. Such challenge to private property and neo-liberalism
was recently echoed in the words of *Laudato Si'*: 'rich and
poor have the same dignity because both of them were made by
the Lord (Proverbs 22:2)'.[11] In contemporary non-theological
language, there was time in quarantine for the realization that
social mobility and equal rights had not become a reality, even
when they had improved, due to the self-interest of those who
owned the resources. I return to the theological and biblical
understanding of the Kingdom of God, whereby all, indeed all,
have equal rights, not only Christians, not only the learned and
the powerful, not only the rich, but the poor. Despite changes
in time and space this led again to alliances between Christians
and movements that supported the same equality values rather
than private enterprise, that is, ecological movements, feminist protests, racial equality forums, LGBT demands. Further,
throughout the pandemic the voice of the poor who could not
feed their children was strengthened, reminding us that despite
equality laws that allow such social mobility, the values of the
Kingdom of God – the now and the not yet – had not been
taken seriously.

Charles Kenny had argued that market growth and the
vitality of empires were in the past regulated by infectious
disease; however, the more contemporary control of disease
has resulted in an urbanized, globalized and wealthy world.[12]
During the pandemic, disease, danger and fear were accompanied by forced lockdowns with military curfew in countries
such as Chile and Liberia, which in turn triggered a crying
isolation. In those cases, there were, of course, many debates
about the plausibility of denying civil rights to large populations through curfews. In the case of Chile, which had had
significant political unrest and violence in October 2019, the
government was accused of exercising undue political power in
order to prevent any social unrest within a response to Covid-
19 that was slow within a country in which very quickly there
were more people unemployed rather than employed.

It was within such a global development that, at least in Latin
America, the voice of the theologians was absent. As I will

outline later, the old-fashioned worker priests were the only ones who appeared on television challenging measures against the poor and having an influence that very few contemporary bishops could have claimed. The Chilean bishops were silent and, unlike the Jesuits, the Archbishop of Santiago was not seen walking among his people. Pope Francis remained the most important religious leader who managed to gather faithful Catholics around a real online daily reflection on how the gospel could guide our daily actions within an unprecedented time of uncertainty, crisis and death.[13] An initial analysis of such a pandemic from the point of view of a theology of the poor erased the idea of capitalism as saviour and challenged past intellectualized discourses in liberation theology without the poor.

I am referring here to the plausibility that arose at the beginning of the twenty-first century that liberation theology, already declared a system of fundamental concepts by Jon Sobrino and Ignacio Ellacuría, could be developed as a system of thought rather than a reflection on God and society from the standpoint of the poor.[14] I am not disputing here the natural development of liberation theology within a very gifted first generation of liberation theologians, including Sobrino and his liberating Christology, and Ellacuría who not only challenged the mere existence of a theology without history and without ethics but got killed by Salvadorian soldiers in the process.[15] However, 30 years after such a development was criticized by Marcella Althaus-Reid, I would argue that in a rethinking of the theology of the poor we need to challenge any paradigms of establishment. What followed the publication of systematic concepts and a large publishing development was certainly a theological disassociation of the theologies of the poor between trained theologians and the communities who were at that time just coming out of years of martyrdom.[16] Thus, during the military regimes in Latin America, theologians in Brazil, El Salvador, Guatemala, Peru, Chile, Uruguay and Argentina made challenging theological narratives that advanced the possibilities of a church of the poor.[17] The Jesuits in El Salvador continued such theological development but the increasing secularization of Latin America created a public perception of a possible 'death of liberation theology' and a revival through academics in Europe and the United States.[18] I would argue that, as Latin America searched for prosperity within democracy in the 1990s, the poor became marginalized even more because they were poor and they didn't have even a return to democratic governments to look forward to. It is true that the attack on liberation theology by Cardinal Ratzinger was relentless, but there was an ongoing dichotomy between doing theology and writing theology. Those considered liberation theologians at the beginning of the twenty-first century were actually writing theology from universities rather than from shanty towns.

With hindsight in the case of Latin America, the Christian communities underwent a great challenge within democracy and secularism from the 1990s because there were other voices and other spaces for the discourse of social justice and the values of the Kingdom. I ask today, and I include myself: how was it possible to reflect theologically on the poor and the marginalized without them being at the centre of such reflection of 'universal responsibility'?[19] How was it possible not to continue such a close journey with those preferred by God and who could have shown us the very face of God? I make the distinction here between contextual theologies of identity, political theologies of rights and the ongoing theological reflection on God's presence within the local and contemporary world. I am afraid that I return time and again to the theological methodology that distinguishes liberation theology from other kinds of theologies: the action–reflection–action that is different from a pastoral plan through which aims and objectives are first and foremost outlined in order to be implemented. This is the method of a committed Christian who, seeing a suffering person, decides to console that person first, to feed her, to clothe her, and to visit her, while later asking questions about the possibility that institutional policies and state selfishness might have triggered such suffering. I remember an incident that alerted me to the fact that, after a few years in Scotland (I have been in Scotland since 1994),

I was returning each year to a different world. The incident involved one of the Chilean bishops who, years later and after Pope Francis' visit to Chile (2017), had to resign because of criminal accusations in a criminal court for abuse (rape of a minor). Until that incident I had been fully preoccupied by the post Rwanda genocide events; indeed, the year of the genocide (1994) marked the year in which I took an academic post in Scotland, and in 2006 Marcella Althaus-Reid and I were appointed to our personal chairs in the Faculties of Divinity of Edinburgh and St Andrews.[20] On a visit to Santiago I had dinner with the future bishop, 'A', in a Santiago restaurant because we had both studied together in our younger years and were close friends. With enthusiasm, and as I started a period of research on the Church in Chile, I had sent him a flier of my 2002 book that had a chapter on the memory of the disappeared in Chile.[21] At dinner he scolded me for speaking about those topics in theology, and he got so annoyed with me about my understanding of the Church, the poor and the marginalized that he left the table before the end of dinner. I was at that time working on the archives of the Chilean Vicariate of Solidarity at the Archdiocese of Santiago and I was in touch with many relatives of the disappeared who had been supported by the Catholic Church during the Pinochet regime.[22] That was not the case any longer, things had changed, and clerics I knew well were not mixing with communists any longer. Thus, our current challenge in a true revival of liberation theology is to listen to the poor, in a time in which people are hungry, unemployed and frightened, regardless of their political affiliation or their religious beliefs.

The challenge of this ongoing era of post-pandemic liberation theology is of a return to an ecclesial reflection as it was in 1968 Peru and indeed within the meeting of Latin American Bishops in Medellin, Colombia. Liberation theology within an ecclesial body, the Church, could become an empty vessel of utilitarian charity, simply because God is the liberator, and the ecclesial reflection activates the role of the poor within their own agency in the Kingdom of God and in society.[23] The post-idealist theology of Metz in particular, and political theology in general, asked about the action of God and the plausibility of reflecting on such action following a socio-historical study of the facts of life and history.[24] We all became poorer through the pandemic, as happened to the post-Rwanda genocide society. Money could not buy life or security any longer and we encountered each other in that boat of humanity so poignantly spoken about by Pope Francis in an empty St Peter's Square in March 2020. Within this chapter, I reflect on the cries of the poor in different countries, such as India, Chile and Somaliland, and the response of solidarity and humanity that has challenged fear and anxiety with a clear sense that God is not punishing us, but is for once being allowed to walk with us – the crying praxis of Emmaus and the solitude of emptiness replaces and challenges the atonement and the intellectualization of the incarnation.[25] People of all religions find a purpose in helping the needy and cease to feel that they are enemies. It is in such a *Sitz im Leben* that one must understand the new context for theologizing: not reflecting on the period of the first and second generations of liberation theology, that is, the military regimes have gone, together with the effort to bring acceptance to theologies of the poor by a second generation. However, that first generation has been ignored as the poor have been ignored. Thus, in this chapter, as Gutiérrez did in his seminal work, I want to argue that a contextual theology of the poor must be re-discussed by 'inscribing', in the words of Ricoeur, the context in which the poor communicate with God; indeed, the context in which the poor communicate with all their divinities, and the context in which Christian theology must operate in a postcolonial setting.

The Emptying of the Squares

The Covid-19 pandemic as a set of medical emergencies, starting in China in 2019 and arriving in Europe, the Americas and Asia in early 2020 brought from the start a fear of illness. However, the measures imposed by different governments and their efforts to save as many lives as possible, and to avoid a complete economic breakdown, brought a period with emergency instructions of isolation that had only been experienced on such a massive scale in Europe during the Second World War. As in any national or major natural disaster, the initial discomfort was of an individual nature but escalated to the communal fear of not having food or communications or indeed medical help. Here I return to my experience in Chile during this period, which is not like the European experience with a system of social state benefits including health and education. Social benefits in the third world are very limited or non-existent, even within a more prosperous country such as Chile. Thus, within a very complex system of health contributions managed privately, citizens have access to limited benefits in healthcare and need to pay for surgery, for example, according to their plan. Thus, the medical centre that a person attends depends in reality on the money invested in the system and the financial possibilities of a person at any given time rather than on a state policy.

In Chile, the poor and the marginalized attend state surgeries, which have a shortage of medical personnel and medications but at a basic level can diagnose illness and support those who are registered only within the state sector. The same applies for internet facilities, phones and every other commodity that relies on payments to private companies, contracts and income. Therefore, the economic situation of a person dictates the rate of survival within a pandemic in a country in which state care has been improved but is still insufficient. The price of groceries is similar to that of Europe and the money I spent weekly on my own needs was not very different from what I would have spent in Europe. I shall expand on these topics in the next chapter. I recognize that it was difficult for colleagues in Europe to understand when my internet connection was not up to speed, or the fact that several of my neighbours did not have much to eat or money for their medication, or even money to get a phone or internet when everything was available. In 1968, when Gutiérrez wrote A *Theology of Liberation*, he described Chimbote within a context in which there was extreme poverty in Latin America at a state and family level.

Today, Latin American indicators are an image of progress, and Chile's infrastructure in Santiago has been deemed one of the best in Latin America. However, the level of inequality of distribution of resources, education and health means that social mobility is not the norm and that in Santiago many in the population depend on non-contractual jobs. Thus, the selling of goods on the streets as informal vendors is so central to a significant number of the unemployed that when mobility came to a halt with isolation, and with the rest of the measures of confinement, the majority of the Chilean population did not have any means to pay for food and shelter.

In the early years of the development of contextual and liberation theology, Latin American bishops sent some of their brightest priests to study sociology or social anthropology in order to be trained to aid Christian leaders to analyse social situations of poverty and marginalization. Thus, Marxist analysis came into the work of liberation theology, with words such as 'praxis'. Today the same analysis is valid, so that Jesuit universities in Latin America have very competent social scientists, who aid reflection by pastoral agents in order to serve and accompany the people of God. In a way, Pope Francis' latest works, *Laudato Si'* and *Querida Amazonia*, follow such theological analysis of watching reality, then reflecting with the biblical text, and then acting in order to request justice so as to create the conditions for peace in society. In *Laudato Si'*, Pope Francis starts with a sociological analysis of what is happening in 'our house', as he calls planet earth, remembering Francis of Assisi who spoke of the planet as our sister and also as our mother.[26]

The pandemic and the lockdown forced Christian communities and theologians to face the plausibility of the end and the implausibility of the eternal and powerful human who had already perished in every country with the first cases of Covid-19. The physical lockdown brought the closing of churches, mosques, synagogues and temples, with a sense of fear, emptiness and isolation. More of these experiences in the next chapter, and as I write this work, three and a half months in solitary confinement, together with two budgies, it is a fact that one budgie died and didn't survive the lockdown. But the emptiness and self-reflection, the surrounding news of death and lack of commerce, brought to our souls a fear of the unknown because we had become too attached to the known, to our own creation, to globalization as an end rather than a means to an end. Suddenly, returning to the Scriptures, we felt strange realizing that the first Christians waited for the Lord anxiously and didn't understand why he had not returned in their lifetime. For, the possibility of an early death brought the realization that neither resources nor titles nor great ideas would bring an end to the pandemic or would save one's life. Reflections on orthodoxy, on right praise (*doxa*), also had their basis erased as the liturgy couldn't be celebrated in community and the very foundations of our existence were shaken to the core. Were we able to wait for the Lord? Was the Lord at hand as the great Liberator? Was he a Consoler at a time in which we couldn't have the control we wanted at any given moment within our lives?

It was an experience of trust and, theologically, several options regarding the nature, action and care of God were uttered. It is a truism to say that in the Old Testament and in ancient civilizations, as well as most natural religions, pestilence, sickness and death were associated with sin. God was reminding his people that they had sinned and broken the covenant. Thus, war, sickness, death and exile appeared. Such an explanation was not taken as valid by most Christian churches and world religions during this pandemic, but there was a sense in a second explanation that God was remote and that maybe he didn't care about the human race or the animals, or the planets. The rational twenty-first century, through enlightened scientists and rationalists, firmly proclaimed in every piece of news that a vaccine was the only solution and that the scientists were to become the 'saviours of the world'. If hours of news and the browsing of newspapers seemed to give this second hypothesis credibility, an uncertain future event offered no hope. While scientists continued their research, everybody knew that the development of a vaccine can take years. In my ethnographic present in Chile, I stood amused and silent at the announcement that Chile was doing so well that China was starting conversations so that a vaccine could be developed at the Catholic Pontifical University and tested on Chilean subjects. Colonialism had returned, as China, a contemporary colonial power at war with other countries and imposing new laws on security issues in Hong Kong, was now paying a Chilean university in order to conduct experiments on humans that should be conducted by pharmaceutical companies on Chinese and within the People's Republic of China (PRC). In what resembled past experiments by pharmaceutical companies on fertility and cancer drugs in Kenya and India, the poor remained on target as guinea pigs for the enrichment of companies and the safety of those who would be able to afford the vaccines and medications that will come out of these trials. It is in the midst of such turmoil that the voices of two religious leaders were significant, reminding us of the divine life and divine intervention within suffering: Pope Francis and the 14th Dalai Lama.

During March 2020, most of Europe went into lockdown as the Covid-19 pandemic started to spread through major cities and all countries within the European Union. While the pandemic did not respect borders, Christian and Buddhist communities found themselves affected not only in Europe but throughout the world, and their leaders developed a public theology of the global present. The response by Pope Francis was of a global invitation for Christians, and indeed people of all and no faith, to join him in prayer on 27 March 2020.[27] Those joining in their millions witnessed not only the solidarity of a shared humanity but saw Pope Francis standing on his own in St Peter's Square, under the rain and in lockdown, leading a common prayer and delivering a homily in which he spoke about opening our boats to the stranger, to the poor, and to all regardless of their nationality, creed or race. He prayed in front of the image of the Christ who had saved Rome in the past, praying for deliverance, mercy and health for the whole world. His *Urbi et Orbi* blessing to the City of Rome and to the world was received by Christians and non-Christians all over the world. It was the first global event that followed the shock of the pandemic and this author witnessed it in Chile, connected to Buddhists and Hindus from all over the world. It was a moving event in which, under the Roman rain, Pope Francis looked frail and as if he had the world on his shoulders. Later, the Dalai Lama imparted, together with Buddhists and people of all faiths present online from all over the world, the Tibetan Buddhist Avalokiteshvara Empowerment during the mornings of 29 and 30 May (IST) from his home in Dharamshala, India.[28] This was the first time that the Dalai Lama performed a 'transmission of knowledge' online, and with more than a million people connected from different places in the world. Avalokiteshvara is the earthly manifestation of the self-born eternal Buddha Amitabha, whose figure is represented in his headdress, and he guards the world in the interval between the departure of the historical Buddha, Gautama, and the appearance of the future buddha, Maitreya. The Dalai Lama initiated all present on the rituals and transmissions of the blessing known as 'the Lion's Roar' to keep us all safe during the pandemic. Over two mornings, the role of the Bodhisattva was outlined and those present were commissioned to transmit such knowledge to others and to exercise compassion in the world. Interfaith dialogue was realized, and communities came together as never before.

Orthodoxy and Orthopraxy

When I spoke to students of theology in Brazil during the pandemic (29 June 2020) we agreed that there were two misconceptions in the understanding of liberation theology: the first, the acceptance of a caricature of angry theologians taking guns, and the other of established theologians who, in a liberal way, were far from orthodoxy and faith. Liberation theology remains a faith-based theology, that is, faith seeking understanding, in which the empowerment of the poor and the marginalized comes from a life lived and learned from the poor and the marginalized. Regardless, there was still some anxiety about the danger, and a tension between orthodoxy and orthopraxy. Whenever I have heard the word 'danger' I have prepared myself for a frontal attack on liberation theology as a liberal artifice of the end of Christianity as Christendom.

Indeed, if one goes back to the beginnings of liberation theology, and assuming the critique of Marcella Althaus-Reid about male clerics and their clerical world, those clerics were Christians who lived among the poor and who risked their lives for the gospel, rather than being institutionalized theological brains that had arrived because they were able to describe the true God. I note that such a first generation of liberation theologians, as I described using Mannheim's paradox of the problem of generations, were mostly Roman Catholics and therefore with the winds of Vatican II behind them. Liberation theologians of the second generation included women and Reformed theologians, but it has been the case that fewer Evangelical and Reformed theologians could be part of such theological liberation because their theologies could not consider a fully human God. Now we can talk about the third, post-pandemic, generation of liberation theologians.

Orthodoxy as the right praise of God requires a response to the simple question concerning the right praise of God. The answers are as many as the diverse traditions within Christianity. However, the place, role and action of the Christ as the mediator between God and humans remain central to such divisions or what opponents of liberation theology would call tensions. For some, the Christ had already redeemed and chosen the elect at the beginning of time. For Catholics and Orthodox Christians, the Christ was sent by the Father, became a true human being, walked the earth, tried to change the world, and was arrested, tortured and died on a cross. The plan of salvation for liberation theology has not been completed, as human beings are called to be part of the people of God, an inclusive term coined by Vatican II that includes all other human beings, and can journey with God throughout their lives. Then, at the end of life, the 'four things' will take place: death, judgement, heaven or hell. Therefore, in this book I cannot change the plausibility that Christ died and rose from the dead and that salvation came to all, not to a few. I cannot declare myself 'saved', because I am still journeying with God and that God is journeying with every human being within this life, and the next. Orthodoxy becomes an assertion of the power and presence of God, of a compassion and love, that we cannot deny in our theological books. Instead, the call to serve God and other human beings becomes the sign of Christians, so that in serving neighbour, I serve God. Therefore, following the parables of the Kingdom in Matthew 25, the hungry, the naked and the prisoner become the presence of God among us. What is the unclear part within such orthodoxy is unclear to me, but it has been asked many times: why do liberation theologians insist on trying to preach and write about changes in society and of changing society? Because it is in the Gospels, and, for a Roman Catholic, within the tradition and the social doctrine of the Church, as well as in the example of many men and women who have lived the gospel before us – the saints.

Orthopraxis becomes, then, the first step of such theological reflection as praxis. Praxis is not understood as practice, but as the action to live and become like those preferred by God, those in need as in Matthew 25, the poor and the marginalized. This theological choice only becomes radical because the choice in the incarnation becomes God's radical choice for Galileans rather than Romans, and for the poor rather than the well-to-do. Thus, there is no tension between serving the poor and bringing dignity and rights to them and what the gospel and the tradition of the Church have taught us. There is a tension of course if the life of the gospel is an intellectual exercise and if salvation as the free granting and reception of grace is a selfish, individualistic exercise rather than a life in community that serves others, be they Christians or not and particularly those in need.

Thus, as a result of the pandemic, in which we experienced communal solidarity and schooling in the needs of others, the lessons and theological questions are rather different than they were before. Temples, churches and synagogues ceased to become the centres of solidarity because they were locked down. However, as was the case with the first disciples, localized pockets of people were able to look after each other, to sing loudly in between the silence and isolation, and to worry about those who were lonely or infirm and who could not walk to the shops or the pharmacies. This was not a romantic period in life but it reminded us of the human and divine values that we had ceased to appreciate as central within the life of a shared humanity of which we are all part, regardless of religion, race or nationality.

Experience in Liberation Theology

Experience has been at the foundations of liberation theology so that action has become the 'first step' to know God and therefore to write about theology. Experience becomes not only a theological method but the very sense of being human and therefore being able to communicate with God. In European theology knowledge is primarily intellectual because the idea of something allows us to recognize a concept in reality. However, the experience of church from the beginning was an experiential knowledge that became cumulative within the tradition. It is here that the roots of liberation theology, in a group of majority Catholic theologians responding to Vatican II, have weight within the history of liberation theology. The experience of the Divine within the human is a process under-represented within pre-Vatican II theology. Those who tried to humanize theology such as Yves Congar or Pierre Teilhard de Chardin were misunderstood and even ostracized because they were humanizing the Divine to an extent unrecognizable by anyone brought up on the basic idea of a rational and never-changing God. Experience was in the realm of philosophy while theology was the bearer of the Truth. There was never a contradiction between these different manners of writing about God and I would like to argue that European systematic theology is no more than another kind of contextual theology that needs to be studied and respected, but in context rather than as a universalized colonial essence.

Experience becomes central to theology because it is through the experience of the poor in the here and now that we experience an encounter and therefore get to know the Christ. Thus, three types of experience could be isolated within a contextual theology, and liberation theology is a lens within contextual theology: the experience of the poor, the experience of the Divine through the poor, and the writing on the salvific presence of God within the world of the poor, the marginalized, migrants and persecuted. It is plausible that the Latin American theologians of a first generation wrote fewer words about the situation of the poor because they were among them all the time, and once one stays in a socio-cultural context for long one tends to lose the sharpness of the first encounter and the first analysis. Thus, how do we acquire an experience of the poor if we have everything and we have the certitude of a job, medical insurance, a family and a future? I return to ways and means of acquiring this experience in interreligious dialogue and I argue that it is through such dialogue that we leave our certitudes. It is through the encounter with the Other, as well as the great possibilities of the media and the encounter with personal narratives by those suffering, that we acquire the experience of the poor. For, if we live in a literate society, we can witness such experience by a daily sensitivity to the world of the poor and the persecuted through reading the narratives of the poor and the marginalized.

I return to the experience of Pope Francis, who had the experience of the poor when he was archbishop in Buenos Aires but who carefully made choices in order to acquire such experience. For example, taking buses rather than having a driver helped him experience what others in Buenos Aires were experiencing. I note here my theological experiment ten years ago when I took the same bus every morning through the city of Santiago during my sabbatical in order to reflect on the theology of Marcella Althaus-Reid.[29] I had a car and certainly funds for the metro and taxis, but the experience of the bus showed me what people experienced every morning and how, for example, to have a daily newspaper in one's hands was a sign of power and status.

Once Pope Francis moved to the Vatican, he forcefully forwarded the agenda of the poor and the marginalized, of the common home and ecological issues, and indeed started his pontificate with a clear sign: constant movement is a theological position. His first public visit as pontiff was to Lampedusa, the island in southern Italy where so many boats had been destroyed and migrants died trying to reach the safety and protection of Italy and of the European Union. Many of them did not reach the point where, according to the Dublin Protocol, they needed to claim asylum, the first point of entry into the European Union. There, on 8 July 2013, he prayed together with Patriarch Bartholomew for those who had lost their lives and greeted the many immigrants who attended the public Eucharist. The common humanity was not only human but also Christian, as African immigrants started filling pews in parishes and churches, seeking employment caring for the elderly and filling jobs that had long been avoided by young Italians.

On the seventh anniversary of that memorable manifesto for the start of his pontificate, Pope Francis, also confined by the pandemic, celebrated the Eucharist at Santa Marta together with health workers but making a clear point about the significance of such an anniversary during a period of global pandemic. In his homily, Pope Francis remembered his words concerning 'the globalization of indifference' when at Lampedusa he told those present that 'in this globalized world, we have fallen into globalized indifference. We have become used to the suffering of others: it doesn't affect me; it doesn't concern me; it's none of my business!'[30] However, in that search for a personal encounter with the Lord, 'the encounter with the other is also an encounter with Christ', for 'He is the one knocking on our door, hungry, thirsty, naked, sick, imprisoned; he is the one seeking an encounter with us, asking our help, asking to come ashore' (cf. Matt. 25.40).[31]

This is the main characteristic that unites the theologies of liberation as theologies of experience and learning with the theologies of interreligious dialogue. In both types of theology we experience God through others. This kind of encounter has been strange within the pandemic because we have been in isolation. However, within such isolation we have appreciated, we have become more tuned with the feeling of longing to meet others, and in our rare excursion into the public sphere to get food, to go to the doctor or to make a payment, we have sensed a different reality. The beggar and the migrant, the Other and the stranger were part of a multitude in which we journeyed on our own without any possible connection. During the pandemic God made us the people of God together through those moments in which we longed to see another human being. We couldn't meet our parents or brothers and sisters, we didn't go to Church, we didn't experience the togetherness of a job or a football match. But in the midst of that empty city an elderly woman asked for our help, a migrant tried to catch our attention, and a dignified man asked for bread or pasta or a small job in order to have something to eat. The experience of encountering Christ in others was sharper simply because all of us were in danger of being infected and ill, all of us felt the possibility of not having a job, or not being able to return to our desired habits. That fear was inclusive: the poor and the marginalized were there, as Muslims and Hindus and Jews, and migrants and foreigners, as well as citizens.

There is no doubt that the 'see-judge-act' advanced by Paulo Freire, and implemented by José Míguez Bonino and Marcella Althaus-Reid, was superseded by the methodology of 'the preferential option for the poor' advanced by the Latin American bishops in their general meeting in Puebla, Mexico, in 1979. The methodology of 'historicization' of Ignacio Ellacuría in his lectures on history and liberation theology became renewed with epistemological paradigms of experience. 'See' as an experience of admiration and empathy became what Justaert originally called a 'cartography' with the possibility of a 'new materialistic' metaphysics, influenced by Marxism, and in her work grounded in the work of Deleuze, Braidotti and Barad.[32] I refer to her late synthesis because it is one of the few theoretical developments that understood the materiality of experience in liberation theology. Such materiality returns to Lenin's understanding of the development of the state through revolution, described by Marx and Engels after the Paris commune as 'the state understood as the organized proletariat as the dominant class'.[33] In that materiality there is a clear co-creativeness in the social triumph between the state managed by the poor and the marginalized in Lenin and the development of Ellacuría's history through Sobrino's sense of the poor as central within the Kingdom of God. In past terms of the experience of the martyrs of El Salvador – Rutilio Grande, Oscar Romero, Ellacuría and companions – the death of the thousands of peasants and women actualized the Kingdom of God into a liberating victory in which the just state becomes symbolized by the history of El Salvador and the person of Oscar Romero.[34] Gandolfo has outlined the possibility of a hierarchical pyramid in the memory of Latin American martyrdom whereby women were not mentioned within the narratives of martyrdom.[35] Indeed, she is correct in that such hierarchy was very much part of the narratives of victims because Romero, Ellacuría and companions were clerics, but also this was true of the major attacks on the structure of the Catholic Church through its leadership by the Salvadorian Army and security forces. Women have been ignored in their memory, but they too were killed when, as well as men, they 'were living out the option for the poor, the popular church and [were] liberation theologians in El Salvador and throughout Latin America'.[36] For the sake of completion and justice, we name them here through Gandolfo: Silvia Maribel Arriola, María Ercilia and Ana Coralia Martínez, María Magdalena Mónico Juárez, Marianela García Villas, Madeline Lagadec, María Cristina Hernández, Celia Díaz, María Cristina Gómez, Elvira Hernández, Laurita López, Isaura Esperanza, Idalia López, América Fernanda Perdomo, María Rosario Martínez, Patricia Puertas, María Magdalena Henríquez, Elsa Elena Pérez Paredes, Elba Julia Ramos and Celina Maricet Ramos, Ita Ford, Maura Clark, Dorothy Kazel and Jean Donovan.[37]

Returning to Justaert, the 'cartography', the mapping of power and material victory, resides in the preferential option for the poor as a history of salvation rather than as a plausibility of the evolution of a just state. The experience of the poor cannot then be assumed through the 'see-judge-act' of an ethical response, but is the experience of becoming one with the poor and marginalized. It is the experience of opting for the poor, rather than seeing, that realizes the liberation of the poor vis-à-vis the Kingdom of God. The transformation is not educational, but personal; it is a full option for God and her Kingdom; it is the liberating experience of freedom after the challenge of leaving one's ego and selfishness in order to be like those despised in society. Thus, it is a learning experience from the poor, and within the pandemic it has been the learning experience of losing control in solidarity with those who, unlike theologians, did not have any control over their destiny within the state in the first place.

I note here the complementary choice arising from the poor that connects Romero or Ellacuría with the option of priests such as Antonio Llidó and Gaspar García. Both of them were part of a group of Fidei Donum priests, priests on loan to Latin American and African dioceses, who saw poverty, understood it as opposed to God's will, opposed it, were persecuted by the authorities, and later decided to join guerrilla movements as priests.[38] In the case of Gaspar García, who died in Nicaragua on 11 December 1978, he made a conscious choice to offer himself in sacrifice, as Christ would have done, because he didn't have a wife or a family. He didn't see any other choice for impoverished peasants whose underage daughters were taken by landowners and raped. Thus, over a family dinner, after returning to Spain, he said goodbye to his family because he knew that joining the guerrilla movement was a priestly option and he joined them as a priest. Ernesto Cardenal, the Nicaraguan poet and Minister of Culture in the Sandinista government, recognized that he was a Christian who had followed the sacrifice of Christ for others with the same end, being killed for political reasons. However, if one looks at Oscar Romero of El Salvador or the Jesuits killed at the Central American University by Salvadorian soldiers, they followed the same path. Gaspar García, Antonio Llidó and Ignacio Ellacuría could have sought refuge at the Spanish Embassy and been taken safely back to Europe. They did not do so because their experience of the poor and the marginalized brought them to experience Christ and his life in full.

Thus, the experience of God through the poor and the marginalized is not an intellectual experience related to abstract knowledge about figures and data about the poor, but it is an experience of the presence and action of God. God not only provides elements of ethical behaviour but comes to theologians and ministers, and indeed to those who acknowledge suffering through the poor. It is a contextual theology, a practical theology in Scotland's terms, that as a reflection comes out of the crying of the poor and the marginalized. A crying praxis follows the orthodoxy of acknowledging that God is with us among the poor and those who suffer. This theological paradigm is what we have forgotten, when liberation theology has become a theology of solving problems, of aid for the sake of alleviation, and Eucharist for the sake of propitiation. I can only remember that conversation with Gaspar García when I was exiting Nicaragua. I was a minor, my dear Arlen Siu had been killed, and frightened and traumatized I was heading for the Costa Rican border. I returned to help with the harvesting of coffee and the literacy campaign but at that moment Gaspar aided our retreat, remaining there with the 'people of God'. The broken limbs and the bloody wounds are not part of the romantic Spanish painters, past and beautiful; they are real because they are part of the Body of Christ. Eucharist is meaningful because, like the disciples at Emmaus, we have experienced him in the poor and the suffering peoples around us. Later, I was to experience the complete desolation of foreign missionaries being evacuated from Rwanda on to planes for Europe, with the help of the Belgian paratroopers. However, those same Belgian paratroopers were tortured and killed by Rwandan Government soldiers in Kigali while they tried to save the life of the Prime Minister.[39] The choices of the Kingdom of God are not human choices; the experience of Christ in the poor brings liberation and social justice, but sometimes at the expense of one's life. Thus, our experience of Christ is the experience of Christ in the poor.

Why has that experience been considered so political? Simply because of a theological foundation that traditionally emerged out of European societies in which theologians, mostly male clerics, occupied positions of authority within churches, seminaries and faculties of theology, and many abused such power. The martyrs for the Kingdom I have mentioned kept their allegiance centred on a clear equation between the Kingdom of God and the poor, a real commitment to service within the life of the poor, usually messy, usually blessed. Indeed, the experiential time of theologians during the Second World War brought out the life of the worker priests in France and the example of those clerics and lay people who opposed in conscience the mass killings by the Nazi regime and brought a new sense of what God expected of his followers. Through those experiences the Church encountered workers, Marxists, atheists and humanists, without considering them the ultimate enemies of the Church. The experience of working with the poor gave a new sense to the Christian commitment to the people of God, to all who suffer: for example, the experience of eight women from Ontario, Canada, who worked in Latin America after Vatican II, and some of them in Peru, influenced by Gustavo Gutiérrez, who took part not only in the service to the poor through a poor-like lifestyle but as their testimonies witness to:

Ella, Edna, Noreen, Judith and Penelope reflected on how their learning about, and embracing of liberation theology manifested in their social justice practices while serving in their respective mission countries, be it through boycotts of companies deemed corrupt, protests against state repression, or outreach and advocacy for racial and gender equality.[40]

It is this experience that I would like to rekindle in those who call themselves theologians of liberation or who feel close to that experience of a prophetic Church. It happens that the Covid-19 pandemic brought new challenges and the post-pandemic brought unemployment and therefore hunger and insecurity. Within countries that are rich economically such post-pandemic will be felt less, in that education and health are secured as state benefits, but in the majority churches outside Europe and North America the poor will not be a percentage of the temporarily disadvantaged but the majority of citizens. Reasons for such economic reality are not only global and could be understood within the discourse of liberation and economics of the late 1990s. However, the main reason for such economic instability is that the underdeveloped and emerging countries, labelled as middle income or low income in the world charts, have a large number of their population who rely on temporary employment or are simply street vendors and hourly-paid workers on a daily search for temporary employment without state benefits.

Our own personal experience of the world is limited to our own experience in the synchronic, with some diachronic sense of a linear progression, so that we cannot grasp the socio-political realities of the poor if they do not affect us on a daily basis. Our experience of church also conditions how we think, and it is radically different if we become involved with the poor and the marginalized. After all, our theology confirms or challenges our experience of the poor. Moreover, one central question in theological terms dominates our possibilities as theologians: does my ecclesial theology allow for a God who is a liberator, or is my image and doctrine of God that of an unchangeable divine being? Is my image of the Christ that of someone who has already made everything acceptable in the past because he did everything on the cross? Or is God a very close divine person who walks with those she defended through the plan of salvation in the biblical text? Can God change or does experience not matter? All these questions and answers determine in which way God can act in the world, because hundreds of different Christian traditions have developed through such diverse experiences of God and rely on a diversity of theologies arising from such varied experience.

One interesting contribution to the links of education with liberation theology has been Peter McLaren's work on the pedagogy of insurrection, work that has linked the roots of liberation theology in Freire's *Pedagogy of the Oppressed* with an ongoing 'critical pedagogy'.[41] It is through this model that a more universalistic rather than contextual base for liberation theology has emerged.[42] Iconoclastic reflection on the tools, means and objectives of education aid the comprehension of the poor and the marginalized even when their methodology could remain a textual reflection on the ascesis of the great champions of the poor such as Dorothy Day. Indeed, McLaren's call for a process from resurrection to revolution points to an important fact of the pandemic: those in education have been gripped by money and capitalism. Not only is the right to education badly mediated by payments whereby social mobility cannot take place because of social economic differentiation. Indeed, the whole project of good employment and good salaries through education has evolved into corporate consumer managerialism to the point where the human spirit and critical transformation have been greatly attacked. Nevertheless, McLaren's authority is spotless, as he participated in the landless workers' movement of Brazil, the Zapatistas in Mexico, with the Bolivarian Revolution in Venezuela and with insurgent partisans in Colombia and South Africa. His work returns to earlier questions of Latin American theologians, such as Pablo Richard, on the figure of Jesus not only as a socialist but also as a communist. The 'corporeal carnality' of Jesus in the historical work of Enrique Dussel brings a closer connection with 'insurrection' and 'revolution'.

It is such critical fire that one needs after the pandemic in order to question, to reject and to assess critically any actions in the name of global concerns that could work against the dignity of the poor and the marginalized. The poor are made in the image of God and God has a lot to do with a post-pandemic world, and a pre-pandemic revolution in the spirit of the Kingdom of God. The materiality of Matthew 25 is a manifesto of a shared humanity in which God loves the world again and particularly those who suffer. Such reflection brings us to the experience of meeting the poor, of being with them, as I will describe in the following chapter, as useless bystanders who want to learn and want to convert to those values of the Kingdom. This is the kairos of a post-pandemic. Some of us decided on 8 July 2020 to form a group of those who will sit and learn from the poor, the persecuted, the migrants, through an international Network of Liberation Theology and Interreligious Dialogue. If previous generations changed the reflection by Christians and made possible ecumenical alliances, today and after the pandemic we must sit, walk and act together with brothers and sisters of other faiths, of indigenous religions, of no religion, humanists and atheists. This is not the time of apologetics for 'truth' but of the realization of God's reign that includes everybody, and of Christ's presence as the avatar and the embracer of all, because God so loved the world, not part of the world or part of society.

Experience and the Supra-structure

If one returns to the 'ungodly' alliances of Christians and Marxists during the beginnings of liberation theology as a written corpus in the 1970s and 1980s, such experiences of cooperation came together very easily. Not only were the critical challenges to the state at that time occupied by the military common, but the action of liberating spaces with the poor and the marginalized became a much-needed development. In Christian terms, the Kingdom of God in the biblical reflections of Sobrino and others was above the state, particularly an unjust state; however, the Kingdom had a dual tension, 'the already and the non-yet'.[43] Within the already, the servant Church supported cooperating with others, among them Marxists. Marxism in its initial discourse rather than the badly implemented totalitarian practices of Eastern Europe, advocated a social analysis in which the supra-structure, the owner of the means of production, was to be superseded by the infra-structure, that is, the workers and those who worked for the supra-structure. Marx, in his London exile, was not able to articulate an armed revolution, but Engels and Lenin forwarded principles of Marxism that were connected to violent armed struggle. However, as we have already discussed, within the followers of the gospel there was also a group that advocated that through words nothing would change and that 'the already' needed an armed struggle. Indeed, Spanish medieval theologians had already followed principles of a 'just war' in order to advocate the end of a tyrant and a dictatorial state. Those principles were used by Christians involved in the armed struggle in Colombia, such as Camilo Torres, priests and Christian communities in El Salvador, and priests who became ministers after the triumph of the Nicaraguan revolution that deposed Anastasio Somosa in July 1979.[44]

As a liberation theologian I am not interested in arguments for or against such armed options because, as has already been clear in history, Christians have opted in their majority for a peaceful change as advocated through the Catholic Church in the social doctrine of the Church.[45] However, I do respect those who took the path of arms because they did it in conscience, returning to that absolute primacy of conscience advocated by Vatican II. This was the case of theologians of the first generation, such as Pablo Richard who, in supporting Allende's government in Chile, advocated the important role of workers and the proletariat, and of Ernesto Cardenal, who was involved in the attack on the presidential palace of Somosa's father and who in Solentiname made history with his community's reflection on the Gospels.[46] Those reflections clearly made such Gospels alive with the interpretation that the Jesus of the Gospels was a revolutionary who eventually was killed by the Romans for political reasons.[47] I can recall priests and nuns who became part of the revolutionary armed struggle in Latin America, such as Rafael Maroto in Chile who was arrested for being a spokesman of the Movimiento de Izquierda Revolucionario (MIR) under Pinochet's regime, and many Christians, men and women, who joined revolutionary movements because they felt that this was their call in relation to their vocation to build the Kingdom of God.

I will return to these unexpected alliances later in this work precisely because the relation of liberation theology and inter-religious dialogue has not been properly explored. It has been a relation based on the infra-structure, in the communities of the poor and the marginalized, where Christians and Muslims, Hindus and Buddhists, have stood together in order to feed the hungry, to complain about unjust processes within society, and to challenge the state about basic rights such as the rights to clean water, food, housing, education, a clean environment and lately the care of our 'common home'. Ecological issues have become the trench where Christians of all denominations, Marxists, humanists and feminists, have come together in order, for example, to protect Amazonia as a place of universal importance, and the people, nature, culture, forests and sentient beings within it. Within such ongoing developments the writings of Leonardo Boff on the importance of the land and God's creation have been consistent over several decades, and Pope Francis has been at the centre of very forceful theological thinking related in general to the planet and in particular to Amazonia.[48]

It is here once again that we have a new universal movement in which liberation theology in the contemporary scene can perform a liberating praxis and through action develop a new body of theological writings and international meetings. For I have argued previously that when at the start of the twenty-first century questions were asked about liberation theology's status, those asking such questions had not realized that the scene had changed and that Christians were involved in processes of liberation within Christian communities and NGOs, human rights organizations and Fridays for Future, and also governmental organizations. For example, our December 2019 conference on *Laudato Si'* in Santiago, Chile, prepared part of the deliberations of the 2019 United Nations Climate Change Conference (COP 25) in Santiago, which was later moved at the request of the government of Chile to Madrid, due to the violence in Chile from 18 October 2019 onwards.[49] Within the conference, reflections on *Laudato Si'* were connected to the actual liberating praxis of the participants, and the care of the planet became a central issue for the host and organizers, the Milarepa Foundation for Dialogue of Chile. Liberation theologians were present at the meetings of the non-governmental organizations, critically engaging with the lack of process in the care of the planet by the governments involved in COP25, through the movement Civil Society for Climate Action (SCAC).[50]

The cooperation with others in the name of the poor and the

marginalized, and from the perspective of the gospel, was common within the first generation of liberation theologians where even Gustavo Gutiérrez presented his thought on the poor and liberation to the World Bank. Within the same generation Ernesto Cardenal served as Minister of Culture within the Sandinista government, and all of them were extremely active within education and social projects, for example the Jesuits of the Central American University who wrote not only on issues related to the Church and politics but also on agrarian reform and public health. In a later generation, Marcella Althaus-Reid and others took part in the meetings of the World Economic Forum precisely because their reflection was becoming disassociated from the praxis and actions for justice of the Christian communities in the southern hemisphere. The exploration of such experience of praxis becomes the important nexus between seeking the Kingdom of God and contemporary events like those within my own pandemic experience in Chile during 2020, the subject of the next chapter.

Notes

1 World Food Programme, 'Covid-19 will double number of people facing food crises unless swift action is taken', 21 April 2020, at www.wfp.org/news/covid-19-will-double-number-people-facing-food-crises-unless-swift-action-taken, accessed 31.8.20.

2 James Fallows, Vivek Wadhwa, Pico Iyer, Rolf Potts, Elizabeth Becker, James Crabtree, Alexandre De Juniac, 'The Future of Travel after the Coronavirus Pandemic', Foreign Policy, 13 June 2020, at https://foreignpolicy.com/2020/06/13/travel-tourism-coronavirus-pandemic-future/, accessed 31.8.20.

3 In Chile, for example, webpages that assessed hunger and connected those needing food started to appear during the pandemic. See 'Hunger in Chile', at https://lavozdelosque sobran.cl/hambre-en-chile; and 'No More Hunger in Chile', at www.nomashambre.cl, accessed 31.8.20.

4 José Aldunate L., 'El hambre en Chile', at http://josealdunate.cl/img/n253_507_El%20hambre%20en%20Chile.pdf, accessed 31.8.20.

5 The main activities were coordinated by the NGO 'Hogar de Cristo', which had been founded long before Vatican II by the Chilean Jesuit St Alberto Hurtado.

6 www.humandevelopment.va/en/vatican-covid-19.html, accessed 31.8.20.

7 Gaudium et Spes, § 1 outlined the concerns of the Church for the joys and suffering of all, not only those who were members of the Church, while *Populorum Progressio* outlined the right concern of the Church for the development of all. Lately Pope Francis has affirmed such universal responsibility with the stress on a universal communion (*Laudato Si'* § 89–95). For if the earth belongs to all, then the natural mediations of a pandemic that is a universal phenomenon affect all and therefore are of concern to the Church.

8 www.humandevelopment.va/en/vatican-covid-19/gruppi-di-lav oro/gruppo-5.html, accessed 31.8.20.

9 www.humandevelopment.va/it/vatican-covid-19/newsletter/economics.html, accessed 31.8.20.

10 Mario I. Aguilar, 'Pope Francis and the XIV Dalai Lama: The Role of Global Religious Leaders during Covid-19', in Irfan Raja, Ruth Dowson, Abdul Basit Shaikh and Ivan Cohen (eds), *Interfaith in the Age of Coronavirus: A Comparative Examination of Faith Communities' Responses*, London: Bloomsbury, forthcoming.

11 *Laudato Si'* § 94.

12 See the insightful analysis by Charles Kenny, *The Plague Cycle: The Unending War between Humanity and Infectious Disease*, New York: Scribner Book Company, 2021.

13 It is a fact that Pope Francis is the leader of 1.3 billion Catholics throughout the world; thus his power of influencing people around the world remains significant.

14 Ignacio Ellacuría and Jon Sobrino (eds), *Mysterium Liberationis: Fundamental Concepts of Liberation Theology*. Maryknoll, NY: Orbis, North Blackburn, Australia: Collins Dove, 1993.

15 Jon Sobrino SJ, *Where is God? Earthquake, Terrorism, Barbarity and Hope*, Maryknoll, NY: Orbis, 2005, and *No Salvation Outside the Poor: Prophetic-Utopian Essays*. Maryknoll, NY: Orbis, 2008. Ignacio Ellacuría, *La lucha por la justicia: selección de textos de Ignacio Ellacuría (1969–1989)*, ed. Juan Antonio Senent, Bilbao: Universidad de Deusto, 2012; and Michael E. Lee, *Ignacio Ellacuría: Essays en History, Liberation, and Salvation*, Maryknoll, NY: Orbis, 2013.

16 Jon Sobrino SJ, *Companions of Jesus: The Murder and Martyrdom of Salvadorean Martyrs*, London: Catholic Institute for International Relations, 1990.

17 Gustavo Gutiérrez, *We Drink from Our Own Wells: The Spiritual Journey of a People*. Maryknoll, NY: Orbis, 2003.

18 By the early twenty-first century those academics outside Latin America and the third world were the ones influencing publishing houses and the global discourse on the poor, with a strong centralization in Orbis Books, but also those by Reformed theologians without

a southern hemisphere experience. See Miguel A. De La Torre, *Doing Christian Ethics from the Margins*, Maryknoll, NY: Orbis, 2004, and *The Politics of Jesús: A Hispanic Political Theology*, Boulder, CO: Rowan & Littlefield, 2015.

19 Mario I. Aguilar, *The 14th Dalai Lama: Peacekeeping and Universal Responsibility*. London and New York: Routledge, 2021.

20 Marcella Althaus-Reid died on 20 February 2009 due to illness, at a moment when her best theological work was yet to come; see the obituary at www.eswtr.org/en/start/in-memoriam, accessed 31.8.20. Her funeral took place in Edinburgh with her Argentinian family present, as well as her British husband. I was supposed to attend and read a text in Spanish; however, the grief we all felt was so overwhelming that under medical advice I didn't attend. That was maybe the moment when liberation theology lost momentum for a while.

21 Mario I. Aguilar, *Current Issues on Theology and Religion in Latin America and Africa*, Lewiston, NY, and Lampeter: Edwin Mellen Press, 2002.

22 That period of archival research led to several publications, including Mario I. Aguilar, *Amor y una máquina de escribir: La vida de Marcela Sepúlveda Troncoso 1955–1974 / Love and a Typewriter: The Life of Marcela Sepúlveda Troncoso 1955–1974*, Santiago, London and New York: Fundación Literaria Civilización, 2010; *Amor y revolución en la vida de Muriel Dockendorff 1951–1974 / Love and Revolution in the Life of Muriel Dockendorff 1951–1974*, Santiago, London and New York: Fundación Literaria Civilización, 2010; and *Architect and Planner for the Chilean Poor: A Biography of Leopoldo Benítez Herrera 1936–1973*, Santiago, London and New York: Fundación Literaria Civilización, 2011.

23 Leonardo Boff, *Jesus Christ Liberator: Critical Christology for Our Time*, Maryknoll, NY: Orbis, 1978.

24 Johannes Baptist Metz, *Faith in History and Society: Toward a Practical Fundamental Theology*, London Burns & Oates, 1980; *A Passion for God: The Mystical-Political Dimension of Christianity*, New York: Paulist Press, 1997; and *Poverty of Spirit*, New York: Paulist Press, 1998.

25 Eamon Duffy, *Walking to Emmaus*, London: Burns & Oates, 2006; and Denis McBride, *The Road to Emmaus: A Journey from Easter to Pentecost*, London: Redemptorist Publications, 2018.

26 *Carta Encíclica Laudato Si' del Santo Padre Francisco sobre el cuidado de la casa común (Laudato Si')*, 24 May 2015 § 1.

27 'Pope announces extraordinary Urbi et Orbi blessing', *Vatican News*, 22 March 2020, at www.vaticannews.va/en/pope/news/2020-03/pope-calls-for-christians-to-unite-in-prayer-for-end-to-pandemic.html, accessed 31.8.20.

28 www.dalailama.com/videos/avalokiteshvara-empowerment, accessed 31.8.20.

29 Mario I. Aguilar, 'Quelle and Liberation Theology: Theologizing in Twenty-First Century Latin America', in Lisa Isherwood and Mark D. Jordan (eds), *Dancing Theology in Fetish Boots: Essays in Honour of Marcella Althaus-Reid*, London: SCM Press, 2010, pp. 219–27.

30 Pope Francis, Visit to Lampedusa, 'Homily of Holy Father Francis', 'Arena' sports camp, Salina Quarter, Monday, 8 July 2013, Vatican City: Libreria Editrice Vaticana, 2013.

31 Pope Francis, eucharistic celebration to open the meeting of reception structures, 'Liberi dalla paura'('Free from fear'), Fraterna Domus of Sacrofano (Rome), 15 February 2019.

32 Kristien Justaert, 'Cartographies of Experience: Rethinking the Method of Liberation Theology', *Horizons* 42/2, December 2015, pp. 237–61; and *Theology after Deleuze*, London and New York: Continuum, 2012.

33 V. I. Lenin, *El estado y la revolución*, Buenos Aires: Longseller, 2007, p. 61.

34 Jon Sobrino, 'Los mártires jesuánicos en el tercer mundo', *Revista Latinoamericana de Teología* 16/48 (1999), pp. 246–8.

35 Elizabeth O'Donnell Gandolfo, 'Women and Martyrdom: Feminist Liberation Theology in Dialogue with a Latin American Paradigm', *Horizons* 34/1 (2007), pp. 26–53.

36 O'Donnell Gandolfo, 'Women and Martyrdom', p. 29.

37 O'Donnell Gandolfo, 'Women and Martyrdom', pp. 26–7.

38 Mario I. Aguilar, 'Desde España a Chile y Nicaragua en tiempos de revolución: los sacerdotes Fidei Donum 1970–1980', in Natalia Núñez Bargueño and José Ramón Rodríguez Lago (eds), *Redes transnacionales del catolicismo hispánico contemporáneo*, Salamanca: Universidad de Salamanca, 2020.

39 Mario I. Aguilar, *Critical Perspectives on Genocide, Ethnic Cleansing, and Mass Burials. Part I: The Killing of the Belgian Peacekeepers (Rwanda, April 1994)*, Santiago: Fundación Milarepa, 2020.

40 Christine Gervais and Shanisse Kleuskens, 'Beyond their Mission: Solidarity, Activism and Resistence among Ontario-based Women Religious Serving in Latin America', *Etudes d'Histoire Religieuse* 85/1–2 (2019), pp. 73–98 at p. 80.

41 Peter McLaren, *Pedagogy of Insurrection: From Resurrection to Revolution*, Bern and New York: Peter Lang, 2016.

42 Peter McLaren and Peter Jandric, 'From Liberation to Salvation: Revolutionary Critical Pedagogy Meets Liberation Theology', *Policy Futures in Education* 15/5 (June 2017), pp. 620–52.

43 Jon Sobrino, *No Salvation Outside the Poor: Prophetic-Utopian Essays*, Maryknoll, NY: Orbis, 2008.

44 Teofilo Cabestrero, *Revolutionaries for the Gospel: Testimonies of Fifteen Christians in the Nicaraguan Government*, Leuven: Peeters, 1986; and *Camilo Torres: Revolutionary Priest – His Complete Writings and Messages*, ed. John Gerassi, London: Pelican, 1973.

45 Pontifical Council for Justice and Peace, the Vatican, *Compendium of Social Doctrine of the Church*, London: Burns & Oates, 2005.

46 Pablo Richard, *Apocalypse: A People's Commentary on the Book of Revelation*, Eugene, OR: Wipf and Stock, 2009.

47 Ernesto Cardenal, *The Gospel in Solentiname*, Eugene, OR: Wipf and Stock, 2020.

48 Leonardo Boff, *Toward an Eco-Spirituality*, Chestnut Ridge, NY: Crossroad, 2017.

49 COP25 was held in Madrid from 2 to 13 December 2019 under the presidency of Chile, https://cop25.mma.gob.cl, accessed 31.8.20.

50 Sociedad Civil por la Acción Climática (SCAC), at www.porla accionclimatica.cl/, accessed 31.8.20.

2

Conversion and a Post-Pandemic Theology

This chapter is a personal reflection during the pandemic in Santiago, Chile. It is three months into the pandemic and I have returned to my diary. A diary is a theological work in itself, simply because reflections and narratives about God appear, disappear and are inscribed according to the developments of the reality and unreality of God in the world. Theology, as 'faith seeking understanding' in the words of Anselm, is an ongoing exercise that has been at the centre of liberation theology. Diaries of prison were an example of such a search for God in prison via letters, while others such as Pedro Casaldáliga wrote their theological diaries of daily encounters with God through creation in poetry.[1] For Casaldáliga, Ernesto Cardenal summarized the encounter between God and her celestial narrative in the beauty of nature, and Casaldáliga was even questioned when arrested by the Brazilian military about his possession of a copy of Cardenal's book of psalms, a book that was also forbidden in Nicaragua under Somoza.[2] While Teilhard de Chardin managed to inscribe such textual reading on earth/matter and the eucharistic celebration of thanksgiving through earth, Cardenal argued consistently that 'love is not only personal but political, planetary and even cosmic'.[3] In isolation one returns to the basic tools of approximation and theological reflection that one has acquired through a journey of faith. I am sceptical of theological journeys without faith, simply because theology as a science seems to be an apology to other academic practitioners of one's inability to disentangle the material and the immaterial, the human from the Divine, and it is a colonial journey of cleverness rather than a journey of faith together with the people of God.

I have already outlined my critique of the closeness of Petrella and Althaus-Reid with a north American sense of the outer normative or non-canonical to describe the God of liberation. I return to the first generation of liberation theologians who through their faith in a liberating God read Vatican II's 'signs of the times' and marched in renunciation and personal denial along a difficult road against conservatism and racism in the Church, capitalism in the world, and the destruction of the planet, long before any movements of protest rooted in the twenty-first century. Their writings and their speeches became diaries of faith in a God who could challenge the establishment by affirming the primacy of the poor already asserted not only by a biblical understanding of the Kingdom of God but by the Latin American Bishops' Conferences of Medellin (1968) and Puebla (1979). Previously, the search for the work and place of the Church in the world had dominated the reforms proposed by Vatican II, particularly through *Gaudium et Spes*, the Pastoral Constitution on the Church in the modern world. For the document triggered the actions of many by stating at its very start that 'the joys and the hopes, the griefs and the anxieties of the men [and women] of this age, especially those who are poor or in any way afflicted, these are the joys and hopes, the griefs and anxieties of the followers of Christ'.[4]

The pandemic brought me personally to the place where I had started my journey of faith and my theological journey after secondary school. The BBC World Service, in its programme *Reflections on Faith in a Global Crisis*, described my return journey as 'a man finds himself by chance in the country he fled as a political prisoner as the virus spreads and he is trapped'.[5] Indeed, I was trapped with God and myself, and the three budgies. I recalled the times living among the poor in 1980s Pinochet's Chile, and the longest time I spent on my own and in silence at Loyola Hall, Liverpool, the Jesuit retreat house, in 1985, when I took part in the Ignatian Exercises of 30 days in silence. As part of my spirituality, God's words were branded on me by listening to narratives of death and resurrection in the Santiago shanty towns; the experience of the 30 days retreat written by Ignatius of Loyola made me into a reflexive person who never again saw the division between theology and life. The Fifth Week of the Exercises in which I was sent into the world to love God and neighbour was never so poignant as with the pandemic. As it was in the case of Rwanda or Somalia previously, I could not physically take a plane out of the situation and relatives were not of any use because we were all in isolation in different zones of the city. It was the same scenario as on the day of my eighteenth birthday when I left my mother's home in order to join the novitiate of a missionary congregation. With the music of the St Louis Jesuits again playing loudly but softly, I sat crushed in my Santiago flat, cornered by the Lord to reconstruct that Fifth Week long forgotten.

If you pass through raging waters ... If you walk among the burning flames ... you shall not be harmed ... know that I am with you through it all.

Those were words that were sung at my priestly ordination and at every sending.

And blessed are your poor for the Kingdom shall be theirs ... for one day you shall laugh ... Blessed, blessed are you.

The words of my monastic promises at St Aloysius Church, Edinburgh, in 2010 resounded as well. That time with less trumpets and close friends at hand, my promises were to become a hermit and to be with God. In the words of St Romuald, 'Sit in your cell and wait for God.' And God came through the storm of the pandemic. God was not the cause of the pandemic, but radically shook our sense of being in absolute control of the world. And my diary became full of entries related to the poor and the marginalized because around me there was hunger, disease, fear and solidarity. Jobs were lost through the lockdown, and the poor retreated from their public spaces and were locked in Lord Cochrane Street, near the power of the presidential palace but far from the securities of the rich and the powerful. Hunger and unemployment are different in the UK because there are some social securities and because there is a rich economy that can rebuild free education and free health care. Instead, in Lord Cochrane Street I learned again and was taught by the poor and their daily narratives. This was not a romantic visit or a summer experience but the real thing. My theological diary speaks of a very poor theological work without a library, but it aided my understanding of great theologians such as Jon Sobrino, Ignacio Ellacuría, Kabasele Lumbala and Aloysius Pieris. Through their words the experience that requires liberation returned: the conversation with the God who came and is among us. I found Christ as the Liberator in that Venezuelan immigrant who had told me over the years that she was afraid of rain, and there she was standing in front of the minimarket run by Colombians taking the temperature of those intending to enter while she was shivering. All of them commending themselves to the support of the Virgin Mary and hoping for the best with no churches opened and no local church in sight. Communal cooking pots surrounded the place, with hot beans and spaghetti, and lists were made of the old, the sick and the infirm, in order to collect their rubbish and to help with their shopping. I was included, against my will, among the six people most at risk, probably because I was a strange man, buying apples and cornflakes rather than fresh white bread. On the list there was a man who needed dialysis, and those who needed food boxes from the government. At the end of the day there was no chance of making it to the ambulances at night during military curfew; there were no beds in the poorest hospitals, no medicines, no future without jobs and sickness meant the end of sociability, maybe one of the most precious treasures of Latin America, and indeed Africa and Asia. There was no security and no ventilators, there was God.

Within such a pandemic and such uncertainty – I am writing at the peak of sickness and death – the angels were not only the medics and health personnel, as referred to by Pope Francis in his first large open meeting on 20 June 2020, but in the cold winter and under the rain the voice of the Jesuit Refugee Service was a steady reminder that those without a home and without shelter were not forgotten. The Jesuits were prominent in the Chilean media. They spoke publicly on behalf of foreign refugees, demanding repatriation in front of their embassies. Liberation theology was fulfilled on two counts: the poor were respected, comforted and fed, put into buses that brought them to places of safety and quarantine. However, the challenge by the Jesuits was very clear to all: change of economic structures and help for the poor were very necessary – they mobilized many and annoyed many others.

My thoughts and feelings were not kind sometimes:

Diary entry 1

Where is the Archbishop? Every other country had had archbishops blessing people and talking to them. Could the Archbishop say something in the news? It is the feast of Corpus Christi and nothing has been said about the living bread that came from heaven. The Church is being silenced by the powerful and the president upsets many when in his speeches he asks that God may help us.

Diary entry 2

There will be neither hot water for weeks we are told, nor a hairdresser. This is a lesson well learned: only one shirt – I have two pair of trousers and one of them will have to do. The poor are used to this, and they know how to do it without a washing machine and a little bit of water only. So much for postcolonial theology from a well-kept home in Scotland – boot camp for all postgraduates will happen next.

Diary entry 3

'Say to the cities of Judah prepare the ways of the Lord' – this is a good training camp. I myself will shepherd them. A thought that ends when I meet somebody who reminds me that I am on the list of those infirm and at risk, even when I have everything I need. My task: to write and to pray for them.

Diary entry 4

Lights out tonight. The assault by thieves is in my mind. My torch does not work and the three budgies that accompany me are frightened. One has lost its sight and remains in the bottom of the cage. Who will be the next to be intubated? I told them we will not make it to the hospital; pray to the Lord of Birds, and I shall pray to your Creator. Lights returned after shouts against President Maduro of Venezuela and screams from an immigrant community in darkness.

Diary entry 5

The night guard has been taken ill and the day guard has the virus. Kind people who have worked for many years in the building. 'Don Mario, stay in your flat!' – I hear the concerns of others who are on the ground floor while an ambulance arrives. I got gas for my stove delivered and joke that I had gone out without a permit for two minutes.

Diary entry 6

I have not seen any preachers on the street. My view is limited to one window looking at another building. The KLM porcelain houses fill the place and I have copies of books I had left a long time ago, including a full copy of *The Durrells*. Maybe they faced the same situation in Corfu and adapted not only to strange customs but they faced poverty.

Diary entry 7

One of the ladies who keep watch at the entrance to the building was raised in a state home for orphans, then married a military man, and now looks after two children in a rough part of the city. This apartment is like Palm Beach in comparison. She had a face accident and cannot close her left eye. I offered to help, and with the help of two doctors she is given a prescription. She never thought that something could be done. Her face looks better after a month's prescription. She comes to work despite the virus fear. She asked me to help a man who has been made redundant. There is little I can do. She tells me that I am capable of challenging the building administrator. This is to be poor, not to have rights.

Diary entry 8

Horrible smells and choking peppers on the air from the upstairs flat. The Colombians have not played their music for weeks. I fear that they are hiding and that any music will give them away. The rent of my flat is more than a month's salary for most people around me.

Diary entry 9

Colleagues in Scotland worry about my internet connection and I fear for my job, my integrity and my reputation. Indeed, the professor must not be well. I am afraid that the best of BT is not available in this neighbourhood. My PC camera does not work. However, I presume that lack of technology and fear does not count for my postgraduates who seem to feel the whole world should do more for them. I feel solidarity when I speak to my students in India and Malawi and when I attend seminars in Hargeisa, Somaliland. There are a couple of expecting mothers among my graduate students: they are remarkably cheerful, and they understand the situation. A student who has more stability than anybody else complains about my lack of engagement. Difficult to say: I am trying to stay alive. I fear all my support goes to her while the situation is not ideal for graduate studies while it is more than ideal to find God and his Kingdom.

Diary entry 10

Pope Francis and the Dalai Lama have been real troopers with their words, prayers and media every day; I have never felt more supported than when in March Pope Francis stood in St Peter's Square praying for the world under the rain. His theology of the common boat was superb, and if I was his biographer, I became his fan. A real global parish priest because I have not heard from mine – the people in darkness have seen a great light! It was great to complete a work on the Dalai Lama during the pandemic and to be able to join him for the blessing of empowerment with so many around the world. God is light, in her there is no darkness. I can imagine how Thomas Merton would have moaned in a situation like this.

Diary entry 11
I am terrified of ending in the emergency connected to a mechanical respirator. I watched the news and I feel ill. I sneeze and believe that this is the end. Twice I have been bitten by spiders – how do they dare do this? We are in a pandemic and they don't respect my space.

Thoughts on Revolution

I write without stopping to remember the barricades and the reflections on Christ and action of the Spanish priest and guerrilla fighter Gaspar García Laviana, killed by the Nicaraguan National Guard on 11 December 1978. The pandemic brings me to his life and reflections because in a third world country, as in Europe, the pandemic brings not only the threat to life but unemployment, and therefore poverty. The difference is that in Europe health, education and housing are provided by the state, while in the third world they create an inequality where the poor are the main recipients of poverty, unemployment and hunger.

The experience of liberation theology from the side of the poor and the marginalized stopped at the borders of Christianity with very committed Christians creating narratives from the biblical text and from human experience about the involvement of Christians within the safe confines of Christianity. Indeed, the first seminal work, *A Theology of Liberation*, looked to the influential encyclical *Populorum Progressio* written by Paul VI in 1967.[6] In order to further ideas of development relating to theology that Gutiérrez had developed during his years in Lyon, and his view of Latin America after Vatican II, he initially gave a talk to Peruvian priests on the development of liberation theology in 1968. Much later, what was a talk to Catholic priests became a foundational flag of prophetic challenge and social struggle for justice by pastoral agents immersed in the poverty, the violence and the struggle of Latin Americans in the climate of oppressive military regimes. However, the churches remained convinced that the boundaries of Christianity and

Marxism could not be crossed; others such as Enrique Dussel explored such philosophical crossing via ethics and history.[7] Those who challenged these borders were slowly leaving the tenets of orthodoxy and, while feeling the tension with orthopraxis, embraced the narratives of God within an intellectual world in which praxis and liberation didn't seem to fit any longer. Maybe they did, but there is a remarkable difference in style, feeling and commitment between Gutiérrez' *The Power of the Poor in History* and Petrella's *The Future of Liberation Theology*.[8] The context in which such books were written was very different. The Peruvian parish priest managed to write in between piles of papers in a shantytown while the Argentinean son of professional exiles in the United States wrote within the walls of Harvard, looking to a combination of philosophy and law. This is not a thought to undermine theological authority, but liberation theology arises and continues strong out of a real experience with the poor and the writing that comes out not of a transcription of such an experience but of a praxis. Praxis is understood as a Marxist challenge to the supra-structures in which Christianity finds the prophetic will of a crucified Christ who walks the streets today and challenges our sense of a clean and safe God.

Revolution begins inside oneself when one is able to love others who encounter oneself and who have made a significant difference for those who became activists and want to change the world. Liberation from oppression comes not because of a political programme but from the prophetic programme for change, which also requires legislative change, and comes because of a moment in which one is challenged and spoken to by the poor and the marginalized. A hermeneutic of bones, as I suggested previously, in the context of Rwanda, was not a reflection on a sad event that concerned Rwanda, but the bones with their dry flesh and their sense of a decaying humanity were the voice of those who were alive previously on those bones.[9] Within *Theology, Liberation, Genocide*, I earlier explored the deep trauma and suffering of Rwanda through Diop's Murambi, and the response of readers over a decade has been that they were able to empathize with the ongoing suffering of unburied bones.[10] Indeed, several other works have become central to the understanding of Rwanda's suffering and the whole process of human healing and national reconstruction that has taken place; for example *The Bone Woman*, which is a narrative of empathy by a professional forensic anthropologist who worked with human remains in Rwanda, Bosnia, Croatia and Kosovo.[11]

Reading and Developing Empathy

One of the difficult aspects of having a theological post is that very quickly one becomes part of an institutional theology that was not part of Gutiérrez' reality. How does one connect with the poor when one cannot live with the poor because even a simple life in Europe is the life of a person who has the securities of the state? I have had the good luck of having at any given time postgraduate students from the southern hemisphere. Thus, my experience of migration and exile came through the stories of Webster Kameme from Malawi, who was finally forced to leave the UK without protection and who had previously survived political assassination in his home country. The arrival of Kabir Babu from India triggered my intense work on Christian–Hindu dialogue. But there is a problem with the theological experience: I am a male and in most countries of the southern hemisphere males do not interact with females who are part of a male–female divide. I had the same difficulties in my work in Kenya-Somalia, and while I wasn't attacked by female academics it would have been impossible for me to have had any experience of participant observation in the female realm of society. Therefore, what I propose in this pandemic is the possibility of breaching the male–female divide through literature. With Iben Mirreld I had this experience by collaborating together on research in FGM in Sudan, which was done at a distance because it would have been completely inappropriate for me to conduct research in Sudan discussing female genital mutilation.[12] This has been emphasized by Edna Adan of Somaliland, who remembered in her memoirs how taboo the subject was for males, so that when she talked about it in a public meeting of the government of Somaliland such discussion was indeed taking place for the first time ever.[13]

It was Gustavo Gutiérrez in 2004 who encouraged me to reflect deeply on the Church in Chile during conversations at my home in Scotland, but it was Edna Adan who taught me how to theologize. She gave a talk to the African student society of the University of St Andrews on a cold night on the nightmare of FGM and her hospital in Hargeisa, Somaliland, and the students invited me to join them for a drink later. She wanted to talk to me the following morning and it was not easy to say 'no' to Edna, even though I had a very full morning of seminars and a doctoral examination. Finally, I agreed to meet her at her hotel after breakfast, and that led to further conversations on the same morning in between my meetings. I knew very little of contemporary Somalia, and Somaliland, as I had been in Mogadishu in 1992.[14] However, she wanted me to visit and to experience the life of her hospital. She told me that I would never understand suffering or life if I didn't visit. It would have been easier to ask me for a donation, but instead she was asking me to get to know the life of the women and her staff in Hargeisa. Finally, one of my doctoral students arrived there before me, but I thought many times about how to know the reality of the poor when distance and commitments prevented travelling.

It is here that I resume that conversation within the pandemic, the occasion which my Foundation Health Without Borders Chile aided in a very small way the efforts by Edna's Foundation to fund PPE and other supplies for her hospital, which she shared with other hospitals as well. The pandemic left me wanting to be in Hargeisa, and indeed in many other places, but without being able to do so. How does one listen to the poor and the marginalized on occasions when one cannot be there? I developed the practice, and the more general idea of reading biographies or memoirs of the poor and the marginalized. Why biographies or memoirs? Because they are personal accounts, sometimes narrated in the first person, about lives. They can be complemented by human rights reports or development reports, or accounts of domestic violence or oppression and persecution; however, those accounts are personal and emphasize what those who narrate them may want to emphasize. An approximation of such a genre is narrated in my short account of the Babu family of the Punjab, who wanted me to talk about their lives, their hopes and their historical movements through poetry.[15]

I started myself with personal accounts of women victims of violence in the Middle East, a reality I have not experienced. Once again, in my visits to Oman, I was sheltered and protected by a former doctoral student who took me into his family in a way that I could never have imagined. Not even the sun could harm me if he was around, protecting me together with his parents. And I began reading about and experiencing the life of Arab women who had told their stories through autobiographies. In liberation theology I had not written about women, but I wanted to explore the possibility that in theologizing, liberation could be experienced together by men and women of different religions, and in this case by Muslim and Christian women who could teach me about their sufferings and their lives. I started sitting as a student of them, and listened to their words in the text.

Reading Nadia Murad

In the midst of the pandemic I decided to explore new theological authors and discover the narratives of fear, oppression and liberation outside Christianity. Let me read, I said, Nadia Murad, Malala Yousafzai, Hevrin Khalaf and so on. Reading Nadia Murad has all the challenges that contextual theologians have passed on to others, namely, how to convey the voice of the poor and the marginalized without becoming the prominent voice. This conundrum has been mediated in social anthropology through 'participant observation'; however, in theology it has been more difficult to mediate. But let me try to follow texts that were produced with the voice of the poor, and about victims as poor, and that can be checked by readers; they can be read, reread, discussed and interpreted, even with the possibility of sacralizing them. For what I did, and I propose others could do, is to treat these texts as sacred representations of the poor and the marginalized. Texts are read as memorials within theology in which the *zikkaron* (a memorial) allows us to bring the past into the present not only as memory but also as actualization. In anthropology, the past written in texts is narrated within the present and through what is called 'the ethnographic present'. However, these texts become indigenous and sacred voices of the victims because they cannot be changed or appropriated.

Nadia Murad narrates the immediate past and her history within the Yazidi of 2014 in Iraq. ISIS tried to exterminate the Yazidi with a previous 'rational' application of a horrible logic of genocide, which has been summarized by Nadia Murad's barrister: Yazidi, for ISIS, are not believers and therefore they can be enslaved.[16] ISIS attacked Nadia Murad's village and she was sold as a slave. ISIS prepared the Yazidi genocide through their 'Research and Fatwa Department' that studied the Yazidis and concluded that as a Kurdish-speaking group they did not have a holy book and therefore as non-believers they were to be enslaved as an extension of the Sharia.[17] ISIS produced a written guideline on slaves and prisoners, called *Questions and Answers on Taking Captives and Slaves*.[18] Within that *vade mecum*, horrible questions were asked: 'Is it permissible to have intercourse with the female slave who has not reached puberty?' The answer was positive if she is fit for intercourse. 'Is it permissible to sell a female captive?' The answer was positive because they are merely property.[19]

The history and narrative of Malala Yousafzai's attack in Pakistan was very similar. Muslim fundamentalists applied the Qur'an to their own means and ends, stressing the teachings that associate women, and therefore girls, of menstruating age, with the home rather than the public sphere of schooling, learning and future work within Pakistan. Both groups failed to apply the attitudes outlined and implemented by the Prophet Muhammad who welcomed and met people of other religions. In the case of Pakistan there was a tradition of girls educated to the highest level in order to serve God better in their families as well as within society. Nadia Murad's and Malala's histories of terror are like those I heard and experienced in Latin America; they are part of an 'archaeology of knowledge' that once disclosed and opened to humanity become a tool against power and oppression. I raised the same questions in my study of the first book of the Maccabees, in which I asked, maybe naively, what would happen if we assume the history by Josephus is plausible and authentic? [20]

Murad summarized her ordeal and the fate of other Yazidi women in Chapter 8 of her narrative:

> We would be bought at the market, or given as a gift to a new recruit or a high-ranking commander, and then taken back to his home, where we would be raped and humiliated, most of us beaten as well. Then we would be sold or given as a gift again, and again raped and beaten, then sold or given to another militant, and raped and beaten by him, and sold or given, and raped and beaten, and it went this way for as long as we were desirable enough and not yet dead. [21]

Murad has become a well-known author because of her account of her own slavery under ISIS. She was awarded the Nobel Prize in 2018 and her published account of her becoming a slave was introduced by her barrister Amal Clooney. [22] The film by Alexandria Bombach provides some of the semantic and prophetic correctness that I have tried to outline. Within the film, Nadia Murad appears in front of the cameras and the microphones answering questions about her captivity, and her response is different from what we expect. She told the press that the questions she wanted to be asked were not about what happened to her but what could be done to secure the rights of Yazidi people today. [23]

In her Nobel Lecture she had moved on from a personal testimony to represent all Yazidi women in her public request for justice. [24] Her testimony was about the significant change experienced by the Yazidi community as a result of ISIS's genocide on part of the community of Iraq by making women into slaves, killing men, and further by the destruction of Yazidi pilgrimage sites and houses of worship. For Nadia Murad that day in Oslo when she received the Nobel Prize was a very special one, not only for her but for all Yazidi, because 'humanity defeated terrorism' and it was the triumph of women and their children over the perpetrators of crimes against the Yazidi. For her, the hope of the start of peace negotiations was central to her lecture, the start of the protection of women, children and minorities, especially victims of sexual violence. She recalled her dreams of normality and family life before ISIS killed her mother, six of her brothers and her brothers' children. According to her understanding, ISIS wanted to eradicate their religion, which had provided peaceful lives and a society of tolerance for a long time. Iraq, Kurdistan and the international community did not protect them, and while they sympathized with the Yazidi the genocide did not stop, and she maintained that such threat of annihilation is still present. The Yazidi remain in camps and their villages have not been rebuilt while the perpetrators of the killings remain at large.

Her words, strong and firm, resonated in Oslo: 'I do not seek more sympathy; I want to translate those feelings into actions on the ground.' She asked particularly for asylum and immigration opportunities for those who were still in the camps. She considered that day in Oslo important for all Iraqis because she was the first Iraqi to receive the Nobel Prize and because on that day they celebrated the victory against ISIS of Iraqi forces from the north and the south. She spoke about the need to unite to investigate the crimes of ISIS and also prosecute those who welcomed, helped and joined ISIS in Iraq. During 2014, 6,500 Yazidi women and children became captive; they were sold and bought and were sexually and psychologically abused. She warned that if justice were not done a genocide would happen again, and she asserted that 'justice is the only way to achieve peace and co-existence among the various components of Iraq'. Finally, Nadia Murad argued in her lecture that the only prize that could restore dignity to the Yazidi was justice and the prosecution of criminals.

Within the Yazidi genocide and its literature, it is possible to search for an orthopraxis that comes out of a praxis outside the traditional understanding of Christian liberation theology but that opens liberation theology to other religions.[25] For the Yazidi, religion includes elements of ancient Iranian religions as well as elements of Judaism, Nestorian Christianity and Islam. A chief sheikh is their supreme religious head and an emir or prince is the secular head. Their religion had already developed in northern Iraq in the twelfth century. They believed that they were separated from the rest of humankind, being descendants of Adam but not of Eve; thus they have kept to themselves, and marriage outside the community has been forbidden. The Yazidi cosmology describes a creator of the world who, after creating, did not become involved with the world and left it under the control of seven divine beings. The chief divine being is a 'Peacock Angel' who is worshipped in the form of a peacock. An important part of Yazidi worship is played by bronze or iron peacock effigies (*sanjaqs*), which are moved from town to town. An annual pilgrimage is central to their year, in which they journey to the tomb of Sheikh Ádi in the town of Lalish, Iraq. Two books in which they assembled oral traditions during the nineteenth century are central texts for their lives: Kitab al-jilwah ('Book of Revelation') and Mashafrash ('Black Book').[26]

Already, works on Palestinian and Hindu liberation theology challenged an inward-looking sense of Christian identity rather than that of the Pentecost of the Gentiles (Acts 2), with a message and divine understanding in many languages and many sensibilities. In the case of Palestinian liberation theologies, Palestinians have challenged the advance of the Israelites into the promised land, arguing that such an act, understood as salvific by the Jews, became an oppressive action of destruction of other peoples in the name of God. Needless to say, Palestinian liberation theologies have opposed the advance of the state of Israel into what has become known as 'the occupied territories'. In the case of Hindu theologies of liberation, a challenge has been made to the existence and political use of caste as an oppressive system that divides people according to birth and deeds, without allowing for the full equality of Brahma's avatars. And within such theologies a central place has been taken by Dalit theologies, those who are considered unclean and excluded from caste. Praxis becomes a political act and a challenge of orderly structures by the sensibilities of the Kingdom of God. For liberation theologies' tenets are not about rationalities but sensibilities, that is, the sensibilities of the God of the poor and the marginalized. Thus, the reading of autobiographies and personal testimonies provides that liberating praxis that leads to a liberating orthopraxy. Exclusion becomes a central tenet to be challenged and eliminated by the praxis of solidarity and by the liberating statement that God is the God of all, not only of some. Thus, praxis is the action of the human triumph that connects such actions to the incarnational and liberating action of God. Theology then becomes the textual inscription of such liberating action whereby the plausibility of action as praxis in theological terms becomes the equivalent of the action that brings dignity to human beings who have been discriminated against and persecuted. Those powerful oppressors have become powerfully allied with neo-liberal elites that have taken the freedom of the markets as an unjust way of exploiting the poor for their own benefit, as it was in Egypt, Babylon, Jerusalem or Rome within the biblical text.

Learning Peace during the Pandemic

Violence and the absence of peace came into many parts of my pandemic reflections. I recognize that several passages of my life have been marked by an identity of witnessing violence. State and elite violence were always present, and in my pandemic dreams and nightmares they returned. If I go back to my earlier years, I remember awakening to reality when on a Sunday and on my way to my grandparents a young boy put a knife to my throat and asked me to give him my watch. It was a precious watch because my parents had parted from each other when I was two years of age and my father's watch was the only object I had from him, given to me by my mother.

Violence became an opening in which, together with others,

I wanted to understand diverse realities, especially the reality of the poor and marginalized. I fear that the lack of nutrition and education for the poor that triggered such empathy and social compromise in the 1970s is still present in Chile. Children without a home, with mothers struggling to bring meat to the table and feeding them tea and bread, is still a reality behind the façade of a prosperous country. A more just neo-liberal economic system that could work somewhere else where there are resources and a state system, such as that of the UK, France or Germany, has not arrived in Chile. The same large avenues where I was raised are currently being redesigned for better 'social distancing' in a post-pandemic world. However, where I stayed during my quarantine there was no room for two people to walk on the same side of the street, and the post-pandemic world will be that of poverty and injustice. Within such a world of financial puppets and pseudo-Christians wanting their own prosperity, the Catholic Church has remained among the poor and the marginalized, even when it has become a victim of power and lust in scandals of paedophilia and the covering of it by inaction and failure by church authorities.

It is within such a scenario, where I am made angry, by a society so far away from the values of the Kingdom, that I would argue that empathy becomes the route for liberation. The experience of empathy has not been externalized by liberation theology because its prophetic routes were a challenge to social injustice and 'structural sin', and personal empathy was a given by Catholic clergy who were already in the slums of the urban poor. The individual experience of following Christ was downplayed because of its possible association with individualism. Social communal justice was emphasized over individual choices. However, the individual as a catalyst of experiential empathy has a lot to do with structural changes and the end of social injustice, because it is an individual choice for discipleship and a prophetic life that aids any social change. The cases of Nadia Murad and Denis Mukwege, her companion in the Novel Prize Award of 2018, are crucial here. Within a very hard experience of surrounding violence they came out of their own trauma in order not only to denounce social injustice and violence but also to help others and to heal them. They defied the culture of indifference denounced by Pope Francis, and they acted with a liberating praxis without thinking about it: Nadia on the road for four years speaking and denouncing; Denis operating, healing, giving acts of encouragement and acceptance towards victims, one after another. Both of them gave years of their lives to others, in moments in which they could have had reasons not to do so, including tiredness and commitments. Like the saints, and Mukwege has been called one, these icons of liberation acted promptly, and after they realized what they had done they wrote memoirs and personal writings that have helped trigger empathy and compassion in many others.[27]

In the case of Dr Denis Mukwege, he has been nicknamed 'the man who repairs women' because over the past 20 years he has been instrumental in repairing the physical and psychological damage to Congolese women who, as a result of war, have been systematically raped and destroyed as products of war. The main purpose of marching armies in the DRC had been to have resources, be they material or political, but armed groups have terrorized villages and particularly women who have been abused and killed as spoils of war. They have been used to instil fear in others and their wombs destroyed so that descendants of their families and ethnic groups would not reproduce themselves. In a country known as 'the world capital of rape', as I outlined in my work on torture, Dr Mukwege has been a beacon of hope for thousands of women as he has protected them in his hospital and assured them that their dignity and their biological capabilities would be restored, if possible.[28] He founded Panzi Hospital in Bukavu, in the Democratic Republic of Congo, one of the recognized dangerous places in the world, where he became a human rights defender because the victims made him recognize a sad reality: women were used as 'weapons of war'.

In his 2018 Nobel Lecture in Oslo where he received the Nobel Prize for Peace together with Nadia Murad, he not only recalled some of those events that surrounded his life but showed that reflections on action for human lives and dignity were only articulated later on.[29] He told his audience how, on 6 October 1996, rebels attacked the hospital where he was working in Lemera, DRC. Thirty people were killed by rebels, including patients in their beds. They fled, and he set up the Panzi Hospital in Bukavu, where he still works as an obstetrician-gynaecologist today. The first patient admitted had been raped and shot in the genitals. That was the start of thousands of cases that came looking for help and were treated by Dr Mukwege at the hospital. Once babies raped and shot started arriving, he went to the village where they came from and discovered that everybody knew this had happened. Nobody did anything because rebels and authorities were involved. Thus, he went to the military courts and got them convicted. However, such a situation in the DRC has gone on for years, and Dr Mukwege had not only to heal the physical injuries to those women and children's bodies but also to give them shelter and reassure them of their dignity. His words after the praxis of the good Samaritan were clear: 'We all have the power to change the course of history when the beliefs we are fighting for are right.' His contribution was a choice, so that for him 'taking action means saying "no" to indifference – if there is a war to be waged, it is the war against the indifference which is eating away at our societies'. Such indifference avoided action on the report 'DRC: Mapping human rights violations 1993–2003', a report that was requested by the United Nations Security Council after the discovery of three mass graves in the eastern part of the DRC. The mapping team described 617 alleged violent incidents in the DRC between March 1993 and June 2003. More than 1,500 documents were examined and 1,280 witnesses were interviewed.[30] The report is horrific, to say the least, even for somebody like me who has been witness to violence and has read human rights reports over 30 years. In his Nobel lecture, Dr Mukwege called upon the international community to follow the recommendations of the report and to bring to justice those involved in the atrocities, as well as to support a global fund for reparations for victims of sexual violence in armed conflicts.

Praxis and Suffering

In my diary of the pandemic I find myself describing the streets of Santiago, Chile, Lord Cochrane Street, where the events of the pandemic were not part of a fictional narrative or a reconstruction of the plausibility of non-sociability and distancing. Those events were real and brought the sentiments of experience and praxis that made me feel anger, love, fear, passion, intensity, extreme tiredness, and at times made me breathless, anxious and not able to breathe properly.

A Lord's Pandemic (2.7.2020)

I love these people in pandemic
I loved them because they are
Their music is not my music
Their history of migration is not mine.

They have treated me like an old man
They have looked after me without fear
But I have feared them, carriers of corona
Loud dancers at night when silence lives.

I am a privileged human being
With no want but freedom
And the Christ walks around
He smells and weeps and shouts.

There is hunger and pestilence
Rotten teeth because of no water
'Wash your hands' says the government
But there is no water around.

Eight people in a room
But still they want me alone
And the Christ walks towards me
Asking for coins with dirty hands.

Did I get the virus? Why did he get the virus?
I weep when I see the common pots
Of beans and spaghetti and sausage
Hot and steamy for the hungry.

It is winter and it is cold
And it rains in isolation
A body emerges from the stairs
Drunk and smelly looks at me.

A sick person is brought to an ambulance
While the neighbours tell me to get in.
A neighbour is taken. Downstairs.
To another city by plane, no history.

And the hungry Haitians and immigrants
Wonder why they came here in the first place.
To stand in the cold while their children
Wait for food because they don't have any.

I feel hungry and cold all the time
After 3.5 months without a walk
My hair is long, my trousers the same
Do not take two shirts, look at the sparrows.

And it seems that my previous life was a waste.
I dream deliriously and I long for beans on toast
And a pub meal and no poor around me.
But this is praxis, and slowly I am grateful.

I hear the music at night and I fear
They are together, they are contagious
Where is God? God is homeless tonight
In the cold and the night, a hungry person.

Spare me Lord, spare me from hospital
Keep away the dogs that want to kill me
But do not go away because you have come.
¡I love these people in our pandemic!

Vain drops of water

How can I compare history?
I cannot; I have everything
I am on my own, and safe
I have survived and I have a card.

However, a simple drop of water
Coming down from the bathroom
The bathroom ceiling frightens me
Because of the worry of getting help.

Yesterday it rained in the city
Most streets were flooded
Houses inundated, the poor wet
The rivers out of their course.

Once again, I learned from them
Their lives so difficult and tense
But a cup of tea and some hope
Does the trick and makes floods normal.

Disasters present, and mothers
Wanting blankets for their children
Wanting an electric stove and education.
And all that will not come soon.

Because they were born poor
As their parents did,
And their children also.
My daily lesson again.

Pandemic and Immigrants

During my solitary confinement and the pandemic, I went to
buy groceries in two small shops down Eleuterio Ramírez and
Lord Cochrane Streets. By doing so and because at least one of

them was on the ground floor in my building, I didn't have to get a permit from the police – by the end of the pandemic I was only allowed two permits a week. One of the shops was mostly visited by Venezuelans, and one woman who scolded me once because she wasn't Venezuelan returned now and again to her job. She was a cashier in the small store seven days a week, and before the pandemic she had another night job. Another bubbly woman whose job was to check people's temperature before they entered the store, feared rain, indeed the cold, but she was always happy to chat with me about my survival of the Chilean winters. Indeed, I must have looked terribly old to all who were young immigrants. In the second shop, owned by a Chilean woman, they had to translate the kinds of cheese they had and always marvelled that I had gone out. My warm feelings for them grew day by day after I started listening to their stories. A woman who helped at the reception of the building where I stayed had my same surname, something remarkable, and she told me that she came from a remote part of Venezuela where they had very little. She became a cousin.

The number of immigrants to Chile has grown over the past decade because of the pre-pandemic prosperity of the country. However, without the pandemic I would not have had the chance to listen to their lives. It wasn't fiction, it was the cruel reality of people who had left their countries looking for opportunities. If we would only listen to the stories of immigrants to Europe, I thought, we would not have the same distant sense of the nuisance of immigrants from Libya, after their very dangerous journeys through different countries. How distant most people are from those immigrants in Europe – and certainly within theological circles. Maybe one way of understanding 'orthopraxis' would be to read the narratives of the poor and the marginalized as migrants in order to open our hearts to an empathy and metanoia that would bring us closer to Christ, and then closer to the Kingdom's values of justice and peace. Here is another theme to be covered in the contemporary reflections on liberation theology and interreligious dialogue after the pandemic. Migrants suffered enormously during the pandemic because borders were closed and human traffickers and slavers were still active. Human slavery is a contemporary phenomenon as much as a past social sin. Slavery happened in the past, but it didn't stop with legal protections for slaves and today's human slavery is among us.

During my isolation in Santiago I noted with shock in my diary when the evening news reported that a Thai woman, who had been brought into the country by the owners of a well-known Thai restaurant chain in Santiago, had been arrested. The police responded to an anonymous call by a neighbour who had been approached by one of the captive women who had been kept at the restaurant and forced to work without payment and without the hope of returning to their home country. My thoughts went immediately to Pope Francis and his ongoing messages on the plight of humans who are trafficked today. However, the pandemic and the narrative of slavery was not in Libya or on the dark streets of European cities but blocks away from me, here in Santiago.[31]

We face the same clean version of life and the covering up that Pope Francis remembered on the seventh anniversary of his visit to the island of Lampedusa, his first visit outside Rome of his pontificate in 2013. He took time to listen to the stories of migrants who had arrived on the island escaping from political persecution or economic hardship. He remembered that one person had spoken at length and that the translator gave a couple of sentences in his translation. However, that afternoon a young woman who understood the Ethiopian language spoken, and had seen the television when the migrant spoke, told Pope Francis: 'Listen, what the Ethiopian translator told you is not even a quarter of the torture and suffering that people experienced.' Pope Francis, in his anniversary homily, remembered that he exclaimed, 'They gave me the "distilled" version.' Thus, the Pope recognized that what we know about Libya is only the 'distilled version'. And he concluded that 'The war is indeed horrible, we know that, but you cannot imagine the hell that people are living there, in that detention camp. And those people came only with hope of crossing the sea.'[32]

The papal praxis was to visit Lampedusa and to be with the migrants while supporting the local bishop in his work of hospitality towards migrants. On numerous occasions Pope Francis addressed Italian bishops, reminding them of the duty of care towards migrants. The same message was delivered in his visit to Bari in February 2020 when he addressed bishops of the Mediterranean within the meeting 'Mediterranean: Frontier of Peace'. Pope Francis associated the Mediterranean region with those fleeing war or in search of a humanly dignified life. Pope Francis spoke of the attitude of indifference towards, and even rejection of, those migrants through fear of an invasion. Like other leaders such as Khatami the Iranian (see the following chapter), Pope Francis denounced a discourse of a 'clash of civilizations', arguing that 'the rhetoric of the clash of civilizations merely serves to justify violence and to nurture hatred'.[33]

Solitude and Solidarity

It was difficult to be on my own with no possibility of going out – that is, the possibility of walking and greeting somebody, to look at nature and to sense the sea in Scotland. But my existence was like somebody in solitary confinement because those who called me needed something and very few could understand what I was going through. I understood the isolation of the elderly and the fact that poverty provokes isolation, because entertaining in the European sense requires resources. I cried a couple of times, especially when somebody called and only had a couple of minutes and no more, while I expected a longer conversation simply because there was nobody else at the flat to talk to. (Indeed, there was a God who accompanied me.) My thoughts for the BBC World Service expressed it all:

Lord, I am fed up (16.7.2020)

Lord, I am fed up.
Is this what you wanted for us?
Are you walking with us today?
Because we are not walking.
We are stuck inside without permits.

How I long to see you in the streets.
Now four months on my own.
I have taken this time as the desert.
A preparation for what is to come.
As a retreat for the public message
That will follow: You are alive.
You are present in the poor and those who suffer.
Our reliance on prosperity has been crushed.
The values of the Gospel of service are here.
Liberation and the social justice of God are here.

I recognize that every day during the pandemic I suffered from fear: fear of being infected, fear of noise, fear of not having a home on return to Scotland, fear of a car salesman who wanted to come and see me, fear of losing my job, and fear of mental illness. However, during that fear, God was present and I became accustomed to the reality of solitude and loneliness. They were all moments of growth and moments in the presence of God, but with the rational sense that everybody along the corridor was a threat to my health – while I enjoyed a short visit to the local shop I realized how the young were coming closer to me and I ran back to the apartment. We became strangers in our solitude and longed for the companionship that we really did not want to have. We longed for solitude but became aliens to the mere possibility of an individual encounter with God. It was a strange time because there were no witnesses to our journey, and when those witnesses arrived, we realized the beauty of being alone. How I longed for such tranquillity in solitude, but my senses became sharpened by silence so that I heard every small noise as a threatening and awakening bullet that could hit me in silence. Nobody would know if a sudden lack of oxygen or a stroke or a heart attack were to take place, and so many times I reconciled myself to the possibility of death.

Eternal life was a metaphor previously of something remote, but during the pandemic I sensed the sharp claws of the plausibility of death, judgement, heaven and hell. Figures of eternity arrived on the screens and in my thoughts, and I discovered who were the new theologians of liberation and of the prophetic voice of Christ. One of them was Felipe Berríos, a Jesuit priest, who lives in the north in one of the many makeshift houses made of rubbish beside a rubbish heap. He was one of the architects of a successful campaign of housing for the poor, and after pressures from the rich he decided to live with the poor in eastern Congo. When he returned, he settled in the north of Chile, and he truly lives like the poor, speaking of Christ with his own actions of solidarity with those who are considered rubbish by society. My diary reflects his appearance during the pandemic.

Felipe Berríos in TVN. Sober and warm reflection on the pandemic in La Chimba of Antofagasta. No giving of boxes because maybe somebody needs a sanitary towel rather than beans. Small notepads with a certain amount of money to be spent in a local shop. What is the point of accumulating goods if we are going to die? Critical towards the politicians who are taking decisions and blocking the aid to the people despite the fact that their salaries are millions of pesos, thousands and thousands of US dollars.

My reaction: this has been a learning experience of letting it go – we enter the pandemic with fear of no control and dependency on others. Berríos reminded us that the poor are used to that experience of not having control of their lives. We have lost it.

Today there are very few beds left for intensive care. We are in the hands of God and the action/active God does not help our learning experience because we are waiting without knowing what the next step will be. This is an experience of wisdom. This is an interfaith experience because it is the experience that allows us to grow, not by ourselves. The Way of the Bodhisattva chapter 9 talks about what we can do to acquire wisdom.

Practising Wisdom 97, 'So, through training the mind, qualities such as compassion, love, and the wisdom realizing emptiness can be developed.'

I was writing my work on the Fourteenth Dalai Lama and I spent weeks reading and commenting on *The Way of the Bodhisattva*. I realized that within the pandemic our faith was kindled by who we were previously, but at the same time we Christians had the same experience as Buddhists, Hindus and Muslims. There were shared experiences in which we returned to our childhood. Thus, on 16 July, day of Our Lady of Mount Carmel, I wondered why there was a bank holiday in Chile within a climate of secularism. Then I realized that even the most violent attackers of the Church were asking the blessings of Our Lady and following the homage to Our Lady in the north where every year thousands of dancers pay homage to Our Lady. Not this year, when a Mass online was the pinnacle of the popular celebrations.

On 31 March, together with others, I made a promise that has remained confidential until now. On that day I wrote to Eve Parker, one of my former students, and one of the outstanding liberation theologians of a generation, informing her that if there was any doubt about my possible death the following should become clear and public:

I came to Chile on 13 March and found myself quickly within closing borders and with my flight back to Amsterdam cancelled as Argentina closed its borders. I started a period of self-isolation that then coincided with a national state of emergency with night curfew and the military on the streets and a quarantine during the rest of the time without any walks or going out. I have not seen my mother or family as I have been on my own at the building of my Foundation together with three happy budgies. Thus, only God knows when there will be the end of this nightmare and actually planes to return to Europe. Apart from the teaching and supervision, the work I do for the Courts has increased because of the lack of experts and I keep a close eye on Vatican affairs. Thus, days are short and busy. Further, I have been involved in a campaign to help Somaliland through the Edna Adan Hospital in Hargeisa, a place that does not have any ventilators and no trained personnel for the pandemic.

You are the only one who will know about this: with the lack of ventilators in Chile and my asthmatic condition I will probably need to go into hospital if I get the virus. If so, I have told my doctor that if there is a shortage of ventilators the one allocated to me should be given to a mother with children. If this doesn't happen God will guide us through. I have priority and privileges because of my education and past family, the poor don't have it. I would like for one mother to have that ventilator. May God be with all of us! Inshallah!

Theologies and the Future

My reflections during the pandemic also turned to this different world to come. Churches are not normally opened; encounters in order to explore future avenues, be it for pastoral work or theology, will be done mainly online. The world 'online', which was previously regarded as the future, has become what we don't want, that is, a compulsory world. In that compulsory world we long for personal encounters even within our fear, because we have the human need to meet each other in the full sense of the bodily encounter. How telling to argue that the development of theologies of the body could be crushed by the ongoing sense of personal isolation and the fear of encounter. I am writing as somebody who does not believe that this period of social isolation will create a better online world. On the contrary, I have experienced for myself the online discrimination whereby your access to others, immediately or delayed, will rely on your internet server's speed, your means of accessing such online communication, and at the end the resources you have and the country in which you live. Such a globalized and unified world was already divided by one's possible access to libraries not only in person but also at a distance. It is in this ongoing development of first pandemic and second pandemic that my thoughts have gone to the role of liberation theology within the Christian challenge to 'structural sin'. For it is in this structural sense that there are social institutions created by humans that impede the freedom of God's work for the poor and the marginalized. In the 1970s, 'structural sin', affirmed by the Latin American Meeting of Bishops in Puebla, Mexico, appeared as a very simple assessment of social customs and norms that were central to inequality and injustice. At that time the emphasis was put on poverty in Latin America and the social injustice that such historical fact and life-threatening conditions had on the poor. Even when Petrella articulated a theological critique of the lack of economic analysis in liberation theology it was a fact that those working through a theological paradigm of liberation were using analysis by recognized institutions such as the United Nations in order to act within social reality. I return here to that effort by Petrella and Althaus-Reid to make liberation theology relevant within the halls of academia. Indeed, some of us supported it, but at that time none of us had the pastoral credibility of an older generation such as Gustavo Gutiérrez or Jon Sobrino, who had worked close to the poor. In the case of Sobrino, he had survived the impending assassination with his fellow Jesuits at the University of Central America in San Salvador, assassination that he escaped by the fact that he was in Asia at that very moment (1989).

In that context, not only discussions on praxis and orthopraxis become central to questions of liberation theology and interreligious dialogue, but the line between liberation theology as a contextual theology and the differences between types or ways of doing theology become smaller. To take a contemporary pressing example, there is Chinese theology, simply because the position of Hong Kong vis-à-vis the People's Republic of China has become different and difficult in 2020. One must differentiate the diversity of Chinese theology, as competently explored by Chloë Starr, because contextual theology and liberation theology that come close to models of political theologies and public theologies would be asking hard questions about the freedom of religion and the possibility of a real 'institutional sin' by not allowing such freedom.[34] Chinese theologies have been more conservative in relation to building churches, but only recently and with the protests in Hong Kong have become closer to liberation theologies based on praxis rather than on universal ethical principles. Indeed, the discussions on Chinese theology and liturgical rights within the Church have created over centuries a flourishing ground for such distinction,[35] for example, the lectures that Joseph Cardinal Zen delivered in Hong Kong to commemorate the tenth anniversary of Pope Benedict XVI's 2007 'Letter to the Church in the People's Republic of China'.[36] Cardinal Zen had a difficult mediation between a Chinese government that seemed to be opening to the Western world at that time and the reality of an unofficial underground Catholic Church that assumed Communism as the main obstacle in any diplomacy between the Catholic Church and the Chinese government. In my own work with Hannah Smith, we argued that regardless of the possible diplomatic or undiplomatic relations between the Vatican and the PRC, any position on China by the Vatican was required to remember that religious persecution does exist because the state does not provide religious freedom. Thus, the mere act of considering one part of the Catholic Church acceptable in legal terms as being official and state managed, and another part illegal or underground because simply they will not recognize the Communist Party as above the Pope, cannot be acceptable as orthopraxis.[37]

It is within such contextual relations between the state and the churches that the field of political theology arose, suggesting that neither systematic theologies nor practical theologies are unique bearers of a theological method (see the Introduction to this book). Instead, they are theologies of context in which, in the case of systematic theologies, the context of an epistemological development comes from Greek, Roman and European philosophy, while in practical theology the context of such theological reflection does not evolve solely out of context. The epistemological roots of such theologies could be different and any negative argument a colonial argument to be revised. Yes, systematic theology is a European contextual theology. I have already emphasized such diversity in theological method in my work on African theologies, particularly the concrete plausibility of Hegel's ignorance of human epistemology and his dismissal of Africa on colonial contexts of racism and colonialism.[38]

I am not alone in these digressions and the original work by David Wilhite has provided a fresh and original approach to the centrality of patristics, and particularly the African Fathers, in order to understand theological developments that go well beyond the Reformation and provide an earlier development to the diversity of God and her revelation. Hegel was not competent enough to see what Wilhite did, that is, there were Fathers of the Church who were Africans, including Augustine, a work supported by classicists such as Karla Pollmann.[39] Thus, Pollmann's work on the reception of Augustine by different disciplines opened such critical discussion on the person of Augustine and his writings, discussions that moved within an empire larger than just the centrality of Italy.[40]

All these works that I remembered within my pandemic confinement gave me the strength to move forward with further explorations of theologies outside the European episteme, following the massive project on African philosophies led by V. Y. Mudimbe.[41] For Mudimbe provided a very insightful analysis on the formation of a European epistemology that erased African parameters in Africa, and particularly in the Belgian Congo, assuming a project of literacy through missionaries who made possible, through the use of the Catholic liturgy and the biblical text, a colonial project of textuality without African participation.[42] Indeed, Pierre-Philippe Fraiture has managed to organize Mudimbe's opus portraying him as a Congolese philosopher who organized ideas on epistemology as a very fruitful reinvention of African thought.[43] But was it a reinvention or was it Mudimbe's 'creative decision to embrace abstruseness against didacticism'?[44] For Mudimbe, the invention of the world by the Belgian colonizers was not only an economic and military enterprise but a reinvention of a *terra nullius*, of an invented empty land, void of thought, ideas and order, simply because it was not seen like that by a Europe that could only listen to the thought of Hegel about an individual that could never be found within an African empty land. Later research, of course, made such reimagination of Africa different, and the final plausibility of Mudimbe's solitude away from his family turned fully towards his residence in the DRC after a life of being somebody who was denied his African existence.[45]

It was during Mudimbe's visit to the School of Oriental and African Studies (SOAS) in 1990 or 1991 that I was asked to respond to one of his lectures, a lecture on missionaries. Mudimbe was not very fond of missionaries, and the audience included in a small seminar room the figure of Mary Douglas, very fond of missionaries and a convert to Catholicism. It was kind of my doctoral mentors, Professors J. D. Y. Peed and Richard Fardon, to ask me to respond to Mudimbe.[46] My response was published, and I had the great opportunity of speaking alone with Mudimbe over a glass of wine. He was convinced that African thought and Latin American thought had a lot to offer and told me about his process of learning Spanish while teaching in California. However, he spoke of the importance of pestilence and pests, metaphorically speaking, in Africa where Europeans had destroyed the very identity of Africans by simply using literacy as an arm of empire. Had I done so as a missionary, he asked me? I had been a missionary in Kenya from 1987 to 1990. Years later, and as I was elected to serve in the Council of the International African Institute of London, he became president and chaired our sessions with a certain elegance and using flourished French and Latin in order to bring us to the diversity of Africa, including the Flemish and Latin used at the monasteries. However, he reminded me several times of the Christian denial of African thought and the African contribution to a global world, a denial and acknowledgement that came to me during my quarantine.

Such contemporary denial came publicly through a tweet sent by John Milbank, theologian and founder of 'radical orthodoxy', who maybe in an irrational spree, and after all the global support for 'Black lives matter', delivered the following tweet: 'Of course the themed identity theology you mention (liberation, local, 'practice based' black, feminist, queer, trans, disability etc etc) is tiresome careerist and naturally elitist bollocks. But no one serious takes it seriously. Or if they do that is utterly tragic' (@johnmilbank3 12.7.2020). My reply after Anderson Jeremiah's reply on 14 July 2020: 'I am afraid that according to Milbank my theology is utterly tragic, and that of Pope Francis. Anderson let's move forth in orthodoxy' (@MarioIAguilar 14.7.2020). I had invited Milbank to speak at the first colloquium of my newly founded Centre for the Study of Religion and Politics (CSRP) at the University of St Andrews in February 2005, and over a few beers we discussed the ongoing nature of religion and politics. However, in writing my theology of the periphery I decided to read critically his *Theology and Social Theory* and found it wanting better academic preparation and real understanding of the enrichment of the theological enterprise by the use of the social sciences.[47] However, in this case, my response followed simply because I found his comments on social media rather wanting, comments that could be uttered within a closed-door seminar but that outlined the lack of respect for ethnic minorities and their ongoing quest for real equality and accessibility, particularly after protests against statues of slave traders in different cities and universities in the UK. I also thought of the work that in such areas, including disabilities, has impacted my own work and has certainly changed my theological views on many areas that years ago I didn't even think existed; namely, Louise Lawrence on sensory disability in the biblical text, James Morris on historical narratives of identity processing in Japan, and the real voices of goddesses and prostitutes within the lives of the poor and the marginalized in India brought to us forcefully and lovingly by Eve Parker.[48] More on this in the following chapters, but the beauty of God remains in her walking among us as the impermanent Emmanuel. During the pandemic we have suffered, but we have also seen her glory.

I am grateful to the readers and the SCM Press commissioning editor for allowing me to express a variety of conundrums that are essential and foundational for a new perspective on liberation theology after the pandemic. In between the feelings of ineptitude of the pandemic (praxis), I found enormous strength in theological reflection (theology), following the journey of those opened to God's diversity and love for all of humanity through a continuation of this journey for the future (orthodoxy). Thus, in the next couple of chapters, having acted with solidarity with others in my confinement and having reflected on the past that brought me to where I am now, I dedicate myself to a critical learning. I write about learning different ideas and different faiths that have managed to assert the global nature of humanity and the common journey, not only encompassing a diversity of identities but a common search for social justice and universal peace.

Notes

1 Frei Betto, *L'Église des prisons*, Bilbao: Desclée de Brouwer, 2017.

2 Ernesto Cardenal, 'Epístola a Monseñor Casaldáliga', in Ernesto Cardenal, *Poesía y revolución: Antología poética*, Mexico City: Editorial Edicol, 1979, p. 133.

3 Dina Livingstone, 'Introduction', in Ernesto Cardenal, *The Music of the Spheres*. London: Katabasis, 1990, p. 9.

4 *Gaudium et Spes* § 1.

5 John McCarthy, *Heart and Soul*: 'Prayer: Reflections on Faith in a Global Crisis', BBC World Service, 7 June 2020, at www.bbc.co.uk/programmes/w3ctot25, accessed 31.8.20.

6 Gustavo Gutiérrez, *A Theology of Liberation*, SCM Classics, London: SCM Press, 2010, Spanish original *Teología de la liberación: Perspectivas*, Lima: CEP, 1971, English edition original published by Orbis, 1973.

7 Enrique Dussel, *Beyond Philosophy: Ethics, History, Marxism, and Liberation Theology*, ed. Eduardo Mendieta, Lanham, Boulder, New York and Oxford: Rowman & Littlefield Publishers Inc., 2003.

8 Gustavo Gutiérrez, *The Power of the Poor in History: Selected Writings*, London: SCM Press, 1986, and Ivan Petrella, *The Future of Liberation Theology: An Argument and Manifesto*, London: Routledge, 2004.

9 Mario I. Aguilar, *The Rwanda Genocide and the Call to Deepen Christianity in Africa*, Eldoret, Kenya: AMECEA Gaba Publications, 1998; and *Theology, Liberation, Genocide: A Theology of the Periphery*, London: SCM Press, 2009.

10 Boubacar Boris Diop, *Murambi: The Book of Bones*, Bloomington, IN: Indiana University Press, 2016.

11 Clea Coff, *The Bone Woman: A Forensic Anthropologist's Search for Truth in the Mass Graves of Rwanda, Bosnia, Croatia and Kosovo*, New York: Random House, 2004.

12 Iben Merrild and Mario I. Aguilar, *Female Genital Mutilation in the Sudan: The Complexities of Eradication*, Current Issues in Religion and Politics, volume II – Working Papers of the Centre for the Study of Religion and Politics (CSRP), University of St Andrews, St Andrews, Scotland: Centre for the Study of Religion and Politics, and Santiago, London and New York: Fundación Literaria Civilización, 2011.

13 Edna Adan Ismail, *A Woman of Firsts: The Midwife Who Built a Hospital and Changed the World*, London: HQ, 2019.

14 My diaries of Mogadishu remain confidential, but it was a period of civil war in which Somaliland was attacked to the point of genocide by the government of Mogadishu. However, life in Mogadishu was marked by the endless fight between clans distinguished by attempts to regain control of the fish market and with only one period of unification: the landing of 1,800 US marines on 9 December 1992; see Abdurahman Abdullahi, *Making Sense of Somali History*, volume II, London: Adonis & Abbey Publishers Ltd, 2018.

15 Mario I. Aguilar, *The Way of the Hermit: Interfaith Encounters in Silence and Prayer*, London and Philadelphia: Jessica Kingsley, 2017.

16 Amal Clooney, 'Foreword', in Nadia Murad, and Jenna Krajeski, *The Last Girl: My Story of Captivity and My Fight against the Islamic State*, London: Virago, 2017, pp. ix–xi.

17 Clooney, 'Foreword', p. x.

18 Clooney, 'Foreword', p. x.

19 Clooney, 'Foreword', p. x.

20 Mario I. Aguilar, 'Rethinking the Judean Past: Questions of History and a Social Archaeology of Memory in the First Book of the Maccabees', *Biblical Theology Bulletin* 30/2 (2000), pp. 58–67.

21 Murad and Krajeski, *The Last Girl*, p. 161.

22 Murad and Krajeski, *The Last Girl*.

23 Film by Alexandria Bombach, *On her shoulders* (2018). Trailer at www.onhershouldersfilm.com.

24 © Nobel lecture given by Nobel Peace Prize Laurate 2018, Nadia Murad, Oslo, 10 December 2018.

25 Shaker Jeffrey and Katharine Holstein, *Shadow on the Mountain: A Yazidi Memoir of Terror, Resistance and Hope*, London: Da Capo Press, 2020; *Farida Khalaf, the Girl who Escaped ISIS: This is My Story*, New York: Atria Books, 2016.

26 www.britannica.com/topic/Yazidi, accessed 31.8.20.

27 Denis Mukwege with Berthild Akerlund, *Plaidoyer pour la vie: L'autobiographie de 'L'homme qui répare les femmes'*, Paris: Éditions de l'Archipel, 2016.

28 Mario I. Aguilar, *Religion, Torture and the Liberation of God*, New York: Routledge, 2015.

29 Nobel lecture given by Nobel Prize Laurate 2018, Denis Mukwege, Oslo, 10 December 2018, at www.nobelprize.org/prizes/peace/2018/mukwege/55721-denis-mukwege-nobel-lecture-2/, accessed 31.8.20.

30 United Nations Human Rights, Office of the High Commissioner, *Democratic Republic of the Congo, 1993–2003: Report of the Mapping Exercise documenting the most serious violations of human rights and international humanitarian law committed within the territory of the Democratic Republic of the Congo between March 1993 and June 2003*, August 2010, at www.ohchr.org/Documents/Countries/CD/DRC_MAPPING_REPORT_FINAL_EN.pdf, accessed 31.8.20. The original document was written in French and is available at www.ohchr.org/Documents/Countries/CD/DRC_MAPPING_REPORT_FINAL_FR.pdf, accessed 31.8.20.

31 www.indh.cl/corte-de-apelaciones-de-santiago-confirmo-prision-preventiva-para-socios-de-restaurantes-lai-thai-formalizados-por-trata-de-personas/, accessed 31.8.20.

32 Pope Francis, Holy Mass on the anniversary of the visit to Lampedusa, 'Homily of His Holiness Pope Francis', Casa Santa Marta chapel, Wednesday, 8 July 2020, Vatican City: Libreria Editrice Vaticana, 2020.

33 Pope Francis, Visit of the Holy Father to Bari for the meeting of reflection and spirituality, 'Mediterranean: Frontier of Peace', meeting with the Bishops of the Mediterranean, Address of His Holiness, Basilica of St Nicholas (Bari), Sunday, 23 February 2020, Vatican City: Libreria Editrice Vaticana, 2020.

34 Chloë Starr, *Chinese Theology: Text and Context*. New Haven, CT, and London: Yale University Press, 2017.

35 R. Po-Chia Hsia, *A Jesuit in the Forbidden City: Matteo Ricci 1552–1610*, New York: Oxford University Press, 2010.

36 Joseph Cardinal Zen, *For Love of My People I will not Remain Silent: A Series of Eight Lectures in Defense and Clarification of the 2007 Letter of Pope Benedict XVI to the Church in the People's Republic of China*, San Francisco, CA: Ignatius Press, 2019.

37 Hannah Smith with Mario I. Aguilar, *The People's Republic of China (PRC) and the Vatican: Prospects for Rapprochement*, Current Issues in Religion and Politics, volume III – Working Papers of the Centre for the Study of Religion and Politics (CSRP), University of St Andrews: CSRP and Santiago, London and New York: Fundación Literaria Civilización, 2011.

38 Mario I. Aguilar, 'Postcolonial African Theology in Kabasele Lumbala', *Theological Studies* 63/2 (2002), pp. 302–23.

39 David E. Wilhite, *Ancient African Christianity: An Introduction to a Unique Context and Tradition*, London and New York: Routledge, 2017.

40 Karla Pollmann, in collaboration with Willemien Otten and others, *The Oxford Guide to the Historical Reception of Augustine* (*OGHRA*), Oxford: Oxford University Press, 2013.

41 V. Y. Mudimbe, *The Invention of Africa: Gnosis, Philosophy and the Order of Knowledge*, Oxford: James Currey, 1990, previously Bloomington, IN: Indiana University Press, 1988; and *The Idea of Africa*, Oxford: James Currey, 1995.

42 V. Y. Mudimbe, *Parables and Fables: Exegesis, Textuality and Politics in Central Africa*, Madison, WI: University of Wisconsin Press, 1991.

43 Pierre-Philippe Fraiture, *V. Y. Mudimbe: Undisciplined Africanism*, Liverpool: Liverpool University Press, 2013.

44 Fraiture, *V. Y. Mudimbe*, p. 12, cf. ch. 2.

45 Kasereka Kavwahirehi, *V. Y. Mudimbe et la re-invention de l'Afrique: Poetique el politique de la de colonisation des sciences humaines*. Amsterdam and New York: Editions Rodopi BV, 2006.

46 Later, I reviewed his books; see Mario I. Aguilar, 'Review of V. Y. Mudimbe, *Parables and Fables: Exegesis, Textuality, and Politics in Central Africa*', *Journal of Religion in Africa* 25/1 (1995), pp. 94–8; and 'Review of V. Y. Mudimbe, *The Idea of Africa*', *Africa: Journal of the International African Institute* 66/2 (1996), pp. 301–2.

47 Mario I. Aguilar, *The History and Politics of Latin American Theology*, volumes I–III, London: SCM Press, 2007–08, cf. Volume III; and John Milbank, *Theology and Social Theory: Beyond Secular Reason*, 2nd edn, Oxford: Blackwell, 2006.

48 Louise J. Lawrence, *Sense and Stigma in the Gospels: Depictions of Sensory-Disabled Characters*, New York: Oxford University Press, 2013; James Harry Morris, 'Rethinking the History of Conversion to Christianity in Japan 1549–1644', unpublished PhD thesis, University of St Andrews, 2018; and Eve Rebecca Parker, 'The Virgin and the Whore – An Interreligious Challenge for Our Times: Exploring the Politics of Religious Belonging with Tamar', *The Ecumenical Review* 71/5 (2019), pp. 693–705.

3

Theologizing at the Waters

How to theologize after the pandemic? How to be able to recognize God in the narrative we create out of our own frailty? How to narrate action rather than thoughts within the framework of a liberation theology open to other traditions and to the poor? I return in this chapter to some iconic figures from different traditions who have thought about dialogue and cooperation in a process of searching for the common good. If God is to be spoken about in praxis theology through narratives, and if the pandemic is to be a theological awakening, it would be because we have not missed the actual happenings within the pandemic. I recall the experience of Mother Teresa of Kolkata, who arrived in India as a teacher with the Loreto Sisters and taught many Indian girls not only academic subjects but an ethical attitude towards life. One day, feeling isolated by her environment, she decided to request permission to work in a slum. In such an environment she found God and was followed by several of her former pupils who were Hindus not Christians. Regardless of those who saw in her a pious nun, she challenged social structures, fought for the dignity of the destitute, and created change in a sectarian divide between Hindus and Christians.

Theology through the Experience of the Poor

A significant number of books have been written about the theologies of the poor; much less has been written about the poor as agents of theology.[1] Indeed, one of the problems with a European systematic theology is that it requires philosophical training and it excludes experience so that the theologian becomes an agent of divine intervention by the learned and for the learned rather than a contextual interpreter of God's talk.[2] A further implication is that theological education becomes not a diverse, contextual activity but a passing on of social roles devoid of context.[3] I return in this chapter to one of the agonizing questions about liberation theology and theologians of the past 20 years: why have people not embraced such theology? Are there liberation theologians today? Of course, the places where the search was done at the start of the twenty-first century were universities and within the American Academy of Religion. At that time there were some significant theologians of the first generation still in active academic work, such as the late Otto Maduro who was enthusiastic about any revival of liberation theology, and Gustavo Gutiérrez addressed rooms full of listeners who were trying to connect with the reflection on the action they themselves were carrying out in North America among immigrants and those with less privilege.[4] The encounter between Latin American theologians and Hispanic theologians did not bear the fruits expected, simply because the boundaries were clearly set by the front cover of Petrella's book *The Future of Liberation Theology*.[5] The book's front cover had a map of the Americas with images of dead bodies on the parts that corresponded to Central and South America, and with colourful drawings of Walt Disney's characters covering the upper/northern part of the map. I remembered that the first generation of liberation theologians had also met North American theologians in Detroit and had not managed to find a common purpose. If the intellectual purpose was common, the context was different.

Therefore, with such lessons learned from the past, this chapter will keep to the geographical limits forgotten and marginalized by an invented globalization, a phenomenon that has been crushed by the pandemic. Globalization has been a concept that has embraced a full communication and a certain universal opportunity to exchange goods and knowledge with each other.[6] The language of globalization has been English and the communication line of such globalization has been the internet. However, the experience of such globalization has been outlined within the pandemic: communication is fluent according to the speed of the internet server, and there are millions of poor global citizens who do not have the resources or the money in order to buy internet lines, time, or even a computer in their homes. I note that if we take the minimum income in Chile to be about $500 a month, it is a fact that an average family would struggle to feed themselves and pay rent or utilities with such a sum. A laptop for the family would cost about $500, and there will be expenses for an internet connection. Thus, the pandemic has reminded us that if a family has a good salary and a steady income globalization works well, otherwise the poor are marginalized from any globalized community, and social mobility and state solidarity is in the imagination.

Within such communities it has been an accepted phenomenon that while leaders fight over territories or doctrines, families have to cooperate with others. Thus, the shocking reality of the violence within the 1947 Partition of India was the fact that families who had lived together for centuries and who attended weddings or rejoiced over the birth of a child of Muslims were Hindus, or vice versa. The same happened in the case of Rwanda where Tutsis and Hutus had lived together in peace until colonial powers and ethnic post-independent movements stressed their differences rather than their commonalities. It is within such local/global contexts that further reflections between liberation theology and interreligious dialogue must take place, and it is in this chapter that I bring the actions of some global leaders on the issues of a connected and universal journey of responsibility. I would not hide that it worries me sometimes that, due to our own localized and single-group interest, we forget the fact that one group will only have renewed rights and a just life if universal rights apply to all. This issue was brought up by different scholars after liberation theology had been put under pressure by the Vatican in the 1980s.[7] Is liberation theology just about equal rights or obligations, or is it about a larger global commonality in which the figure of Jesus of Nazareth becomes central to understanding a Christian commitment to learn from and not only to defend the poor and the marginalized? In the questioning of Patrick Claffey and Joseph Egan, was liberation theology a movement or a moment within the Church?[8] In my assessment and opening lecture of that conference in Dublin, I argued that it was a movement, and a movement that responded to Vatican II and triggered change, a kairos for the Latin American Church. By default, it influenced the ecclesiology and pastoral outlook of so many Irish missionaries to Latin America who were present at that conference.[9]

It was clear that in several other pastoral milieus, such as in the Philippines, questions were asked about popular movements and theologians on the barricades; for example, Melba Padilla Maggay, who was instrumental in organizing the Protestant presence at the EDSA barricades during the People Power Uprising in February 1986. While she agrees with the possible limitations of people's power, she argues strongly that emancipation and change only takes place within the roots of a society that at its core is religious.[10] Indeed, the example of the Philippines has differed from other societies in Asia, where Christianity is a minority religion while evangelical Christianity is not the majority religion in the Philippines.[11] For her, such popular power would not work within a milieu in which religion does not play an important social role. The role of People Power in the Philippines was a strong motivator for a rethinking of a common ground within the global concerns of the Kingdom, particularly in Africa where Christianity and Islam have been the main catalysts of conflict and violence, and in Asia where Christianity is indeed a minority religion. However, in order to search for further ideas and examples of such Christian universalism, liberation and interfaith dialogue, we must also search for such examples within leaders, philosophers and thinkers of other world religions; for example, the current work by the contributors to *Post-Christian Interreligious Liberation Theology*, 'that are not replicate at all of Christian or Latin American liberation theology'.[12] Indeed, I agree with the contributors to such volumes that liberation theology could be used as a methodology and a critical way of thinking within other traditions outside Christianity. Is Christianity always the problem? Maybe, but in the case of liberation theology, Hindu liberation theologies have already been outlined, with the enormous possibility of a critique of Hindu caste and the social injustices and inequalities of caste as traditionally understood within India.[13] For context matters so much that once Hindus leave India, caste ceases to be the important marker of ethnicity or of religious belonging.[14]

Liberation Theology and Hindu Caste

A good interfaith mutiny, I would argue, proposes the liveliness of Hinduism and Christianity because it is through such abundant mutinies that Brahma becomes once again the principle of all existence and being, despite a limited human social order. I propose to examine some of the arguments advanced by Anantanad Rambachan not only because in previous works I have argued that his contribution within Hinduism could be crucial to future dialogue between traditionalists and liberationists but also because theologies of liberation cut across the seminal concept of liberation in Hinduism, Christianity and especially Buddhism.[15] Indeed, most critiques of Hindu nationalism have suggested that the caste system needs to change on the ground as indeed it is not accepted legally by India, but any change would need more proactive laws of equality not only at constitutional level but at local level. From marriages, jobs and opportunities to honour killings, a great Gandhian revolution in the social order is needed if those critiques are to have their day.[16] Because to have a desire for social change requires the inclusion of groups and social categories such as social marginals and women, who are currently excluded by Hinduism and by Christianity as well. In examining some of Rambachan's ideas, I am arguing that any changes would make Brahma's manifestation more accessible and that indeed would prevent a dichotomy between ritual and politics within the ongoing life of India.

Rambachan's arguments within liberation theology are common to Hinduism and Christianity because liberation theology arose out of the faith and practice experience of oppression by Christians in Latin America, mainly Catholics, and mainly clergy within the 1960s and 1970s. Critical questions from the point of view of those who practised Christianity related to the social order in which the poor and the marginalized did not have an equal place within society and most of them lived in poverty. Within Catholicism they had to make enormous efforts to take part in rituals in between a harsh life in the shanty towns, while the rich had their own private chapels and clergy at their service. Thus, the striking similarities between the plight of those considered ritually less pure or the excluded within Hinduism in the Indian context.

Rambachan recalls in his work how he was attacked by an Indian bishop when at the invitation of the World Council of Churches he attended a meeting in Brazil in 2006. He was attacked as a Hindu who represented an oppressive religion towards the Indian minorities, and the bishop clearly suggested he wanted the end of Hinduism as a tradition.[17] Indeed, Rambachan, raised in Trinidad and Tobago, had heard of such injustices based on hereditary caste and on work specificity, but had not experienced issues of caste within the West Indies in which his family had settled in the nineteenth century and where caste is a domestic topic but not a national one.[18] Rambachan explained his own social self-realization as follows: 'I had to see my tradition through his eyes and understand the source of his pain and anger. The same tradition that affirmed my self-value denied his own. His experiences had convinced him that caste injustice was intrinsic to Hinduism'.[19] Rambachan explained further that, at the time of the so-called Aryan invasion, there was, according to the *Rigveda*, a tension between those who regarded themselves as of noble descent (*ārya*) and the *dasyus*, who were regarded as inferior, lacking virtue and observing different customs.[20] Indeed, the main consequence of such differentiation was that the *dasyus* were excluded from rituals so that by 800 BCE the *āryas* had consolidated their prominent place and had developed a hierarchically structured system (*varna*).[21] Within the *varna*, the *brahmanas* (priests) occupied the top of this social structure, with another three groups in descending importance, *rājanya/ksatriya* (soldiers), *vaiśyas* (merchants and farmers) and *śūdras* (labourers).[22] The first three groups were considered twice-born and, as a result, deemed worthy of celebrating Vedic rituals.[23] Only males were able to go through the initiatory rituals (*upanayana*) and therefore able to study the Vedas. It is not clear if all groups that were excluded were excluded because of their perception of impurity or if some of them rejected inclusion into the *varna* as well.[24]

Rambachan suggests that by the time the Code of Manu (*MDh*) was becoming known, the social role of classes was assumed to be the product of *karma* in a previous life, so that a lower place in the *varna* was given by bad *karma* in the past and could not be altered within the present.[25] By the period between 400 BCE and 400 CE, untouchability was firmly in place so that the groups outside the social order were labelled *asprśya* (untouchables). They polluted villages and food and needed to be excluded because the Vedas were not taught in villages where they resided and they could not eat foods and look at foods without polluting them for the rest of a village.[26] The same applied for foods offered and containers used for Vedic rituals.[27] Untouchables were considered as polluters and defilers together with animals. Members of the 'Scheduled Castes' as described by the Indian Constitution are about 15 per cent of the total population of India, and amendments to their social status have been made (Protection of Civil Rights Act, 1976) so as to comply with the constitutional principles that suggest that 'the state shall not discriminate against any citizen on grounds of religion, race, caste, sex, place of birth'.

However, the main question revived by Rambachan relates to the essence of the untouchables – are they Hindus or are they not? Mahatma Gandhi argued that they were; however, he maintained the social order of the four classes.[28] Others such as the Dalit leader B. R. Ambedkar (1891–1956) argued that the Dalits could not be Hindus because they are not part of the *varna* system.[29] For Rambachan there are two important developments that arguably could advance even more the end of exclusion due to caste of marginalized groups in India. The first one is a self-critical realization of injustice: 'we need to see caste as one historical expression of a system of human oppression and domination, present in many societies, that sanctified itself in the garb of religious validation'.[30] The second one is his own hopeful possibility of a Hindu tradition that can evolve so that 'there is a theological vision at the heart of Advaita that invalidates the assumptions of inequality, impurity, and indignity that are the foundations of caste belief and practice'.[31]

I would agree with Rambachan in that the caste system contradicts the possible manifestation of Brahma in all creation and therefore the non-duality of Advaita restores the characteristics and the intentionality, indeed the double-intentionality of Brahma. There is a comparative similarity between the non-inclusive history of Hinduism and Christianity in that impurity by divorce or for unmarried women has been slowly challenged as a reason for exclusion from the community. Indeed, interreligious dialogue has brought together communities that previously were considered outcasts, for example the Jews of Europe, always seen as secondary citizens by Catholic majority states during the twentieth century. Within Catholicism it has also been difficult to disentangle the practice of the Church from possible changes that would make God more present in the lives of people and within the planet. Thus, the worship of God goes very much together with the service of others, men and women, and with the care of our common planet.[32]

Women, when looked at as inferior or dependent within the *MDh*, do not fit within the role of Brahma in the universe, so that Brahma's manifestation can be fully realized in all humans, in all creatures, and within the whole universe. In Rambachan's understanding, 'if the human form derives its value from *brahma*'s immanence, then it is an expression of ignorance to despise and oppress women who, like men, embody *brahman*'.[33] One could argue that such lesser dignity given to women creates an injustice that contradicts the identity and unity of existence through brahman, which becomes the ethical principle of *ahimsā* (non-violence).[34] Indeed, the *Bhagavad Gita* has clearly stated: 'The one who sees the Lord, as remaining the same in all beings, as the one who is not being destroyed, in the things that are perishing, he alone sees.'[35]

Objections to such a vision in the Upanishads have been that they represent an ideal and not the reality. Indeed, my argument following Rambachan would be that religions and religious traditions are indeed ideals to be realized over time and through a journey within the physical and the metaphysical; however, philosophies or religious traditions have an impact on their followers now and in the material world. Thus, any recognition of Brahma's manifestation should be deemed sacred for males or females. The plausibility of the exclusion of women from prayers or rituals is different from the order within a household that sets the central parameter of understanding within the developments and varieties of Hinduism. Hinduism and its focus on Brahma would become stronger if Brahma was truly perceived within the here and now as all-embracing and all-manifested.

This is another comparative area that allows Hinduism and Christianity to reflect together on the presence of Brahma and of God within the real contemporary world by allowing an understanding of the liberation of those outside the institutional systems. Social-specific roles emerge out of the equality of Brahma's manifestation and neither challenge the ritual role of Brahminic rites nor exclude the possibility that women, and even outcastes, worship the divine manifestations of Brahma because in reality an all-encompassing Brahma is a powerful manifestation indeed of all the universe. While further analyses could be done on women's mutinies about their exclusion from certain Hindu sites and temples in India during the twenty-first century, these areas of purity and impurity regarding Hindu and Christian women, non-Hindus and non-Christians, remain central to the full understanding of a divine presence within contemporary India. At the centre of such understanding must be the Hindu conception of Advaita, the non-duality that permeates the so-called 'ideal' and that is in fact part of a central tenet of dialogue between Hinduism and Christianity. However, as previously argued, liberation through praxis brings, secondly, a theological reflection that becomes stronger because of the dialogue between different religious traditions.

It is in that common dialogue between different traditions

that we find some theological footsteps to follow after the pandemic. Any divisions have not prevented the attack on the virus, and divisions that are perceived as signs of diversity become markers of the Kingdom that I would like to explore in the following section. For a liberating praxis of dialogue and encounter becomes orthopraxis when we understand God's narratives and actions as inclusive, creative and loving. For there is a diverse understanding and a common bridge through the Divinity, in the thought of Raimon Panikkar, a term that is not the same as God. For Divinity in Panikkar contains a certain mystery, with characteristics of freedom, infinity, immanence and transcendence.[36] However, for Islam, the Oneness of God has been a central understanding and revelation of God, which has impeded a closeness between Islam and Christianity. Nevertheless, liberation theology has had a lot to do with an encounter between Christianity and Islam that does not come from theoretical discussions but from a common journey within and together with humanity, understood as an encounter in the One.

Liberation Theology and the Oneness of God

One of the most influential companions of Pope Francis during his pontificate that started in 2013 has been Bartholomew I of Constantinople, the 270th Archbishop of Constantinople and Ecumenical Patriarch since 2 November 1991 (he was born in 1970 in Imbros, Turkey). The companionship between Bartholomew and Pope Francis has been constant, because both enjoy the ecumenical dimension of the Churches of the East and West, but also because the causes that both understand as central are commonly their own. Thus, refugees, migrants and modern slavery were highlighted in their common visit to Lampedusa (2013); their sense of ecology and the care of the planet has been crucial to their writings, including *Laudato Si'* and *Querida Amazonía*. Their first official private meeting took place in Istanbul (2014) but their very close conversations and lunch took place in Cuba (September 2015) when both spent some time together at a moment when Pope Francis was mediating the peace accord between rebels and the government in Colombia, Cuba was opening to diplomatic relations with the United States, and Pope Francis was making official visits to those two countries.

Pope Francis' visit to Turkey (28–30 November 2014) sealed their cooperation and friendship, a visit that included a meeting with the Turkish President, Prime Minister and civil authorities, and a visit to the President of Religious Affairs (all at Ankara). In Istanbul Pope Francis attended an ecumenical prayer event in the Patriarchal Church of St George, followed by a private meeting with Bartholomew I at the Patriarchal Palace. On the second day of his visit to Istanbul, Pope Francis attended the Divine Liturgy in the Patriarchal Church of St George, with an Ecumenical Blessing and the Signing of the Common Declaration. Pope Francis was deeply moved, and he embraced Bartholomew, bowing to him while Bartholomew kissed Pope Francis' head. On that day he visited the Sultan Ahmet Mosque (Istanbul). At the mosque the Pope did not join any other prayers by the Great Mufti, and they prayed standing side by side in their own traditions in silence. This was the custom brought by Pope Francis to all his visits to mosques and prayers with Muslims.

In Pope Francis' visit to Egypt (28–29 April 2017) there was a development in that a logo and a motto were used: 'Pope of Peace in the Egypt of Peace'. Further, a personal video message was delivered in Rome before the visit. The visit was a state visit in that Pope Francis met with the President of the Republic and had a state welcoming ceremony. However, the main invitation had come from the Grand Imam of al-Azhar to participate in the International Peace Conference. In his speech at the conference, Pope Francis stressed the birth and contribution of Egyptian civilization and gave less importance to Islam. Later, Pope Francis paid a courtesy visit to Pope Tawadros II, and a common declaration was signed between the Coptic Orthodox Patriarchate of Egypt and the Catholic Church, with one purpose: an agreement not to repeat the baptism administered in the Coptic Orthodox Church or the Catholic Church when one person decides to change from one community to the other. During his visit Pope Francis visited al-Azhar headquarters in Cairo, where he also prayed in silence together with the Grand Imam of al-Azhar, Ahmed el-Tayyeb.

It could be argued that Pope Francis followed the example of dialogue with and understanding of Islam mediated by Cardinal Jean-Louis Tauran, a French cardinal who was the proto-deacon (2011–14) and President of the Pontifical Council for Interreligious Dialogue (2014–19), and as Camerlengo he announced Bergoglio's election as Pope Francis. Cardinal Touran was very close to Muslims and he drove a full agenda of interreligious dialogue with the Islamic world. He had been a French soldier in Algeria and later he had the experience of the followers of Charles de Foucauld of prayer in the desert. As part of his agenda he attended the annual gathering of different religious leaders in Muscat, Oman, and became a fearless proposer of a dialogue between Israel and Palestine, with the two-state solution as policy by the Vatican. Thus, Pope Francis' first state visit was to Israel, mediated by the Cardinal's close ally, the King of Jordan. Touran was influenced by his meetings and reading of moderate Islamic intellectuals such as Sheikh Abdullah bin Mohammed al-Salmi (Oman) and Seyyed Mohammad Khatami (Iran). Al-Salmi was the main instigator of the interreligious international agenda by Sultan Qaboos of Oman, and Khatami responded forcefully to any theory of a clash of civilizations with his own 'dialogue of civilizations'.

In a retrospective look at history, the contribution of al-Salmi and Khatami can be united with the encounter of Pope Francis with the Grand Imam of al-Azhar Ahmad al-Tayyeb and the signing of the document on 'Human Fraternity for World Peace and Living Together' on 4 February 2019. During 2019 the United Arab Emirates declared the 'Year of Tolerance' and welcomed the Grand Imam of al-Azhar and Pope Francis to Abu Dhabi. On the same 4 February 2019 Pope Francis addressed an interreligious meeting at the Founder's Memorial in Abu Dhabi where he remembered the eighth centenary of the meeting of St Francis of Assisi and Sultan al-Malik al Kamil, as on that occasion he declared that he had come 'as a believer thirsting for peace, as a brother seeking peace with the brethren'.[37] However, Pope Francis reminded those present that 'the enemy of fraternity is an individualism that translates into the desire to affirm oneself and one's own group above others'. Further, Pope Francis spoke about the requirement of human fraternity and of 'the duty to reject every nuance of approval from the word "war"'.[38]

The encounter took place during the visit of Pope Francis to the United Arab Emirates (3–5 February 2019) and has remained a central pillar of our current understanding of a shared humanity in which 'faith leads a believer to see in the other a brother or sister to be supported and loved'.[39] After the interfaith dialogue meeting, they signed the document on *Human Fraternity*. From the start of the document they made clear that such human fraternity needs a public rather than a private expression and that such expression finds a purpose in 'safeguarding creation and the entire universe and supporting all persons, especially the poorest and those most in need'.[40] Both religious leaders provided a liberating praxis by acting on their leadership through reflections on issues that affect a common humanity, and certainly Muslims and Christians, for example poverty, conflict and suffering in different parts of the world. They also isolated issues that could be considered 'structural sin' in Puebla, and that are causes of poverty and suffering: the arms race, social injustice, corruption, inequality, moral decline, terrorism, discrimination and extremism.[41] The document *Human Fraternity* came out of this encounter 'as a guide for future generations to advance a culture of mutual respect in the awareness of the great divine grace that makes all human beings brothers and sisters'.[42]

Human Fraternity opens a series of inclusive categories with the expression 'In the name of' following the opening of the Qur'an, so that the first opening reads: 'In the name of God who has created all human beings equal in rights, duties and dignity, and who has called them to live together as brothers and sisters, to fill the earth and make known the values of goodness, love, and peace.'[43] Thus, the document becomes a joint declaration of good and heartfelt aspirations in the name of

God, innocent human life, the poor, the destitute, the marginalized, orphans, widows, refugees and those exiled from their homes and their countries, people who have lost their security, their peace and the possibility of living together, human fraternity, fraternity torn apart by policies of extremism and division, freedom, justice and mercy, and all persons of good will present in every part of the world. The adherence to the document was not only an unexpected path of understanding but included al-Azhar al-Sharif and the Muslims of East and West, as well as the Catholic Church and the Catholics of East and West. They together declared 'the adoption of a culture of dialogue as the path; mutual cooperation as the code of conduct; reciprocal understanding as the method and standard'. They condemned practices that are not part of religions as expressions of belief in God, including genocide, acts of terrorism, forced displacement, human organ trafficking, abortion and euthanasia. The conclusions of *Human Fraternity* express their aspiration that 'this Declaration may constitute an invitation to reconciliation and fraternity among all believers, indeed among believers and non-believers, and among all people of good will'.

Over the years such liberating praxis in the togetherness of a journey of interfaith dialogue has been taken by Muslims in the global arena, beginning with the former President of Iran, Seyyed Mohammad Khatami.

Seyyed Mohammad Khatami (Iran)

Following earlier works by renowned philosopher Dariush Shayegan, President Khatami introduced the theory of 'Dialogue among Civilizations' as a response to Samuel P. Huntington's 'Clash of Civilizations' theory. After introducing the concept of his theory in several international societies – most importantly the United Nations – the theory gained a lot of international support.

Consequently, the United Nations proclaimed the year 2001 as the United Nations' 'Year of Dialogue among Civilizations', as per Khatami's suggestion. Pleading for the moralization of politics, Khatami argued that 'the political translation of dialogue among civilizations would consist in arguing that culture, morality, and art must prevail on politics'. President Khatami's call for a dialogue among civilizations elicited a published reply from an American author, Anthony J. Dennis, who served as the originator, contributor and editor of a historic and unprecedented collection of letters addressing all facets of Islamic–Western and US–Iranian relations entitled *Letters to Khatami: A Reply to the Iranian President's Call for a Dialogue among Civilizations*, which was published in the USA by Wyndham Hall Press in July 2001. To date, this book is the only published reply Khatami has ever received from the West.

Khatami believes that the contemporary world in which we live is such that Iranian youth are confronted with new ideas and are receptive to alien habits. He also believes that limitations imposed on youth lead to the separation of them from the Iranian regime and calls them into satanic cultures. He predicted that even worse than that, the youth learn and accept the MTV culture. This fact leads to secularized tendencies. In terms of Islamic values, Mohammad Khatami encouraged film-makers to extend the notions of self-sacrifice, martyrdom and revolutionary patience. Thus, when Khatami was the minister of culture, he believed that cinemas were not mosques and that it is necessary to pay attention to the entertaining aspects of cinema, not limiting them to their religious aspect.

Sheikh Abdullah bin Mohammed al-Salmi (Oman)

Another Muslim scholar, Sheikh Abdullah bin Mohammed al-Salmi from Oman, has been instrumental in forwarding the religious tolerance of Oman and the Ibadi sect that over the years has organized many international meetings of scholars and clerics in order to foster interreligious dialogue. When we met in June 2017 in Muscat, the Minister of Awqaf and Religious Affairs, His Excellency (HE) Sheikh Abdullah bin Mohammed al-Salmi,[44] spoke warmly of his past encounters with academics such as Professors Hans Küng and Jon Esposito.

At the meeting, he gave me some of his works and it is within this section that I want to explore some of them because HE not only has combined a life of service within the Omani government but has been a prolific academic who has been invited to speak at significant academic and church venues in Europe. HE was born in 1962 into a family of erudite *'ulema* from the line of Salmi, assuming his ministerial office in 1997 following the drive for religious tolerance and understanding that has been the policy of the Sultanate of Oman since 1970.[45] HE's grandfather, Sheikh Nur al-Din Salmi, was one of the main thinkers behind the revival of religious thought and the study of Oman, while HE's father was a historian.[46] Thus, within a very troubled and violent Middle East, Oman has managed to emphasize the Ibadi principles of religious tolerance, with a government that has been hospitable to other peoples and other religions within a spirit of such tolerance. Thus, the Sultanate has more than fifty linguistic and confessional congregations, Christians, Hindus and Sikhs as well as Buddhists, Sunni and Shia Muslims.[47] In 1997 the Ministry of Justice and Islamic Affairs changed its name to the Ministry of Religious Affairs. Since then HE has been involved in a series of activities, mostly academic, publishing and of an interfaith nature, which have not only made Ibadism known to outsiders but have enhanced the possibility of understanding and cooperation between Muslim and Christian scholars.[48]

His thought on interfaith dialogue has diversified and has considered events that have taken place in the world, such as the attack on the USA on 9/11, developments in US policy, Vatican policy, the blaming of Islam for violence against the USA, and even the unfortunate lecture delivered by Pope Benedict XVI, who used a character portrayal of Islam in the Middle Ages, which angered the Sheikh of al-Azhar, who sent a letter to the Vatican rebuking the Pope. However, through all these speeches, seven of them published in a single multilingual volume, HE, without apologizing, analysed the rise of fundamentalism in the difficult context, for example, of the military.[49]

One of his many important contributions refers to the issue

of violence on the part of Islam. For if one considers many conversations about Islam after 9/11 the issue of jihad as a war against infidels is frequently cited. In general, those who listen to such questions would agree that a religious text could not call to kill, but sadly, as Pope Benedict did, one returns to the Crusades and starts assuming that jihad is a violent war. Not for HE, who includes violence in his discussion of *haram* (those things prohibited in Islam).[50] Even when, as HE would remind us, advocates of violence in the name of religion have another interpretation, for him 'it is also haram to adopt extreme positions aimed at politicizing religion, whatever the supposed excuse might be'.[51] Thus, once the issue of violence is settled as forbidden then the edifice of dialogue and cooperation can be built. For the beginning of such a search for a Muslim is the call by the Qur'an to a twofold approach in the relationship between Muslims and People of the Scriptures. First, there is a call to People of the Scriptures to join Muslims in worshipping the One God (Q. 3:64), and second, there is a call to treat Christians fairly, for 'We believe in that which has been revealed to us and revealed to you; our God and your God is One, and to Him we have submitted [as Muslims]' (Q. 29:46).[52] For HE, this twofold principle comes out of a 'sharing' by Muslims and the People of the Scriptures that brings together another principle: 'people must deal with each other on an equal footing in terms of humanity, dignity and justice'.[53] For HE there should not be superiority between Muslims and the People of the Scriptures, and the worshipping of other lords rather than God would indicate such divisions so 'that none of us shall take others as lords besides God' (Q. 3:64). Thus, equality towards others comes from that submission to God as Muslims (cf. Q. 3:64).

What follows such principles of belief in God and respect towards others is the development of such an approach with a fair representation of the history and creeds of Christian groups that would set markers for a respectful treatment of Christians.[54] Christians showed respect for the Scriptures and carried out good deeds even when 'committing errors in good faith'. However, they were sent messengers: 'We sent, after them, Jesus, the son of Mary, and bestowed on him the Gospel. And We ordained in the hearts of those who followed him, compassion and mercy' (Q. 57:26–27). Christians are called by the Qur'an 'rebellious transgressors'. However, the Islamic 'calling' and Christian proselytizing bear witness to God and involve others 'in divine goodness – basically in terms of the values that both observe'.[55] As a result, and in explaining theologically the strife between Muslims and Christians, HE returns to the wrongness of the forbidden 'seeking of lordship' whereby violence in the name of Islam is forbidden because of the commonality between Muslims and Christians so that the Qur'anic mandate stands firm regardless of history: 'that none of us shall take each other as lords besides God' (Q. 3:64).[56] Another reason for the clash between Muslims and Christians has been their universal spread and their great numbers.[57]

Historically there was a period between the ninth and sixteenth centuries in which a cooperation that almost became a partnership took place between three great civilizations: the Islamic, the Chinese and the Christian-European.[58] It was only after the sixteenth century that the return to the Greek and the Roman imperial eras divided such partnership in the name of expanding empires. However, HE recognizes that European dominance was not only military but cultural and that Christianity as a shaped cultural and Romanized religion became the source of the clashes with other religions as hegemony rejected past experiences of respect and partnership.[59] Thus, as a Muslim scholar, cited without name by HE, said, 'the fact is that it is not the Romans (i.e. the Europeans) that were Christianized; rather, it is Christianity that has been Romanized'.[60]

Colonialism included a process of cultural hegemony on Muslims in Africa and Asia during the nineteenth and twentieth centuries and it was only at the advent of the Cold War and the Second World War that Christian churches contacted Muslim communities worried about the atheist states that were oppressing Christian and Muslim believers. The Muslim response requested a challenge of Western hegemony and moves towards Muslim recognition in Palestine and Kashmir. If different responses were given, HE acknowledges that the recognition of Islam as an Abrahamic religion came with Vatican II (1962–65).[61] Further, the Soviet invasion of Afghanistan brought together a response against Communism by Muslims and Christians. However, the US response included the unfortunate understanding of a 'clash of civilizations' and new tendencies towards hegemony.[62] The perception of Islam as opposed to the West grew with the use of expressions such as the 'Green Danger', 'Clash of Civilizations', and 'Risks of Fanaticism and Fundamentalism'. Western hegemony was associated with the only solution towards Islamic fundamentalism, and the attacks on the USA by al-Qaeda on 9/11 strengthened the possibility that Islam was a risk to the West. For HE, the last two decades have been dominated by a literature and conversation on conflict as if Islam did not have values of openness, tolerance and democracy. In HE's analysis, he suggests that 'perhaps those policies of conflict were the ones that, over the last two decades, led to the delay in imagining and achieving peaceful transformation'.[63]

The possibilities of Muslims and Christians together come, according to HE, from the call to believe and to do good. A system of values for the common good brings common recognition and a system that protects humanitarian issues such as the right to live, the right to think, the right to religion, the right to reproduction, and the right to property.[64] It could be that at the level of the state, or political level, these rights are ignored but at the level of religious and ethical responsibility there are internal motives and commitments that make such deeds good. These commitments, according to HE, 'include intent, freedom, choice, conscious motives and goals'.[65]

For HE, the contemporary world is different from the previous one as great powers such as China, India, Japan, Indonesia, Turkey or Brazil are arising, thus providing a world that is 'multipolar' rather than the 'unipolar' world that creates conflicts and wars.[66] Within this multipolar world Muslims and Christians can work on a common shared enterprise for the world, and HE suggests four points of cooperation:

1 A study to understand divisions is needed, despite unity on belief and a value system. HE suggests that hegemony would most probably be the result of such a study. Thus, a commitment to a value-based system is needed not only from Muslims and Christians from the whole world, with values such as equality, dignity, freedom, compassion, justice, acquaintance, and public good. HE suggests a 'coalition of civilizations' seeking consensus rather than hegemony.[67]

2 A pluralistic set of values for the world requires insistence on differences, recognition, amicability and embarking on religious and ethical values. Humanity for HE aspires to live a universal order with equal and cooperative partners. Such pluralism should include all parties from all continents.[68]

3 Muslims need to review the work of Muslim religious clerics and scholars. Some of this erroneous work has led to 'negative radicalism'. He suggests that followers of the Abrahamic religions cannot deal any longer with old realities but need a new vision.[69]

4 A new vision, proposed by HE, requires Muslims and Christians to rethink, reform and proceed with a new vision towards monotheism, to apply an unexploited economic exchange system, multipolar politics and ethical responsibility.[70]

The contribution by HE Sheikh Abdullah bin Mohammed al-Salmi certainly assembles the possibilities of dialogue at a global level and within the realms of public policy.

Reflections on Interconnectedness

The visits by Pope Francis to Turkey and Egypt have been seminal in furthering the plausibility of religious unity in diversity. Religion is a complex phenomenon that humanly brings the possibility of 'the dialogue of civilizations', 'the dialogue of a shared humanity', and the enormous plausibility of a 'human fraternity'. Thus, documents express a human desire to serve the divine unity and to reflect on the possibilities of a human journey of faith. Pope Francis argues that, in order to dialogue, one party or the other must leave their comfort and journey, just as the founders Muhammad and Jesus did, going to others. They must look for opportunities to share understandings and encounter differences, not with the sadness of incomplete understanding but with the plausibility of a common journey. Therefore, the journeys of Pope Francis have brought other partners into the conversation: pilgrims such as Patriarch Bartholomew.

Thus, the complexity of dialogue assumes that the formality of a theological diplomacy incorporates the contextual action of dialogue between different civilizations; the 'dialogue of civilizations' becomes the competition for God's love in which different manners of approach and of interconnectedness are negotiated. With Cardinal Tauran as an example, the diplomacy of listening and encountering without an immediate response or solution assumes an ongoing possibility of friendship and the sitting together of members of a common family. Indeed, the contemporary Christian–Muslim dialogue has been the most challenging but the most significant, of Pope Francis' papacy. The warmth of unknown partners has become an ongoing visit to friends, and the friends have brought their families, as was the case of the papal visit to Jordan where the King's family waited for Pope Francis in their living room in order to share some tea and sweets. And indeed, Pope Francis has brought his humanity and warmth to this dialogue, and possible partners have responded. Diplomacy has become the centre of encounter so that very recently Pope Francis has indicated that all future trainees at the Vatican academy must spend a year in a context of service with the very poor of this world. I would argue that the journey continues, and I would like to end this reflection on interfaith dialogue as liberating praxis with the words of my mentor, the late Cardinal Tauran:

> After the 'dialogue with the world' of Paul VI, the 'dialogue of peace' of John Paul II, the 'dialogue of love and truth' of Benedict XVI, we have come to the challenge of inter-

religious dialogue as 'dialogue of friendship', announced by Pope Francis.[71]

However, Tauran was also involved as Vatican Secretary for Relations with States in themes that provided a link between the socio-political action of liberation theology and the praxis of the encounter with other religions that were to become central in the agenda of the twenty-first century and the pandemic and post-pandemic. One of them was the cooperation between the different religions in combating human trafficking. In 2002, Tauran presided at the international conference, 'Twenty-First Century Slavery – The Human Rights Dimension to Trafficking in Human Beings'. For that conference, Pope John Paul II wrote a letter outlining his own close interest in this example of structural sin and outlined some of the important matters that were going to be discussed during the conference. The problem and sin of human trafficking becomes an example of the practical connections between faith communities in dialogue, which start by acting on its denunciation through the liberating praxis of action to eliminate human trafficking. As I will argue in the next chapter, issues of interfaith dialogue, structural sin and liberating praxis provide a connection between liberation theology and interfaith dialogue within the contemporary life of diverse communities during the pandemic and post-pandemic.

Notes

1 For a good contribution on the poor as agents of theology, see the work by some of the leading theological figures in Daniel G. Groody (ed.), *The Option for the Poor in Christian Theology*, Notre Dame, IN: University of Notre Dame Press, 2007.

2 I return here to some of my past reflections on the role of the theologian within the churches and within the politics of a secular and diverse society; see Mario I. Aguilar, 'Public Theology from the Periphery: Victims and Theologians', *International Journal of Public Theology* 1/2007, pp. 321–37.

3 See, for example, the work of the reshaping of the theological curriculum in the Church of England, particularly Mike Higton, *A The-*

ology of Higher Education, Oxford: Oxford University Press, 2012; and Eve Rebecca Parker, 'The Virgin and the Whore – An Interreligious Challenge for Our Time: Exploring the Politics of Religious Belonging with Tamar', *The Ecumenical Review* 71/5 (2019), pp. 693–705.

4 For a later synthesis of Gutiérrez' life and writings, see Robert McAfee Brown, *Gustavo Gutierrez: An Introduction to Liberation Theology*, Eugene, OR: Wipf and Stock, 2013. Otto Maduro was part of a Latin American exiled generation in the USA who never lost his own sense of the dances, songs and smells of a Latin America he portrayed so well. However, he ventured into the areas of liberation and interreligious dialogue before any of us thought about it; see Otto Maduro, *Maps for a Fiesta: A Latina/o Perspective on Knowledge and the Global Crisis*, New York: Fordham University Press, 2015; and *Judaism, Christianity, and Liberation: An Agenda for Dialogue*, Eugene, OR: Wipf and Stock, 2008.

5 Ivan Petrella, *The Future of Liberation Theology: An Argument and Manifesto*, London: SCM Press, 2006.

6 See new developments through the writings of Heiner Flassbeck and Paul Steinhardt, *Failed Globalisation: Inequality, Money, and the Renaissance of the State*, London: World Scientific, 2020; and Finbarr Livesey, *From Global to Local: The Making of Things and the End of Globalization*, New York: Pantheon Books, 2017.

7 Mario I. Aguilar, 'John Paul II and Theologies of Liberation', in Gerard Mannion (ed.), *The Vision of Paul II: Assessing His Thought and Influence*, Collegeville, MN: Liturgical Press, 2008, pp. 144–58.

8 Patrick Claffey and Joseph Egan (eds), *Movement or Moment? Assessing Liberation Theology Forty Years after Medellin*, Berlin: Peter Lang, 2009.

9 Mario I. Aguilar, 'The Kairos of Medellín 1968: Towards a Movement for Liberation and New Mission after Vatican II', in Claffey and Egan (eds), *Movement or Moment?*, pp. 9–28.

10 Melba Padilla Maggay, *Rise Up & Walk: Religion and Culture in Empowering the Poor*, Eugene, OR: Wipf and Stock, 2016.

11 Peter-Ben Smit, *Old Catholic and Philippine Independent Ecclesiologies in History: The Catholic Church in Every Place*, Leiden: Brill, 2011.

12 'Introduction' to Hussam S. Timani and Loye Sekihata Ashton (eds), *Post-Christian Interreligious Liberation Theology*, London: Palgrave Macmillan, 2019.

13 Anantanand Rambachan, *A Hindu Theology of Liberation: Not-Two is Not One*, Albany, NY: State University of New York Press, 2015.

14 Jai Parasram, *Beyond Survival: Indians in Trinidad and Tobago 1845–2017*, Watton at Stone: Hansib Publications, 2018; and Alexander Rocklin, *The Regulation of Religion and the Making of Hinduism in*

Colonial Trinidad, Chapel Hill, NC: University of North Carolina Press, 2019.

15 Rambachan, *A Hindu Theology of Liberation*; see also Rambachan's general holistic vision of Hinduism in his larger works, *Accomplishing the Accomplished: Vedas as a Source of Valid Knowledge in Sankara*, Honolulu: University of Hawai'i Press, 1991; and *The Advaita Worldview: God, World, and Humanity*, Albany, NY: State University of New York Press, 2006.

16 Manpreet Kaur and Mandeep Kaur, *Honour Killings in India: A Crime against Humanity*, New York: Anamika Publishers, 2015.

17 Rambachan, *A Hindu Theology of Liberation*, pp. 167–8.

18 Rambachan, *A Hindu Theology of Liberation*, p. 168.

19 Rambachan, *A Hindu Theology of Liberation*, pp. 168–9.

20 Rambachan, *A Hindu Theology of Liberation*, pp. 169–70.

21 Rambachan, *A Hindu Theology of Liberation*, p. 170.

22 Rambachan, *A Hindu Theology of Liberation*, p. 170.

23 Rambachan, *A Hindu Theology of Liberation*, p. 170.

24 Rambachan, *A Hindu Theology of Liberation*, p. 170.

25 Rambachan, *A Hindu Theology of Liberation*, p. 170.

26 Rambachan, *A Hindu Theology of Liberation*, p. 170.

27 Rambachan, *A Hindu Theology of Liberation*, p. 170.

28 Rambachan, *A Hindu Theology of Liberation*, p. 175.

29 Rambachan, *A Hindu Theology of Liberation*, p. 175. Dr Ambedkar (1891–1956) advocated the equality of untouchables in society and the reform of Hinduism. He led campaigns for equality by, for example, marching with Dalits to draw water from the Chavadar Lake at Mahad, in Maharastra. Dalits drank the water that was later avoided by high-caste Hindus; see Bhimrao Ramji Ambedkar, 'Speech at Mahad', 25 December 1927, in Wendy Doniger (ed.), *Hinduism*, New York and London: W. W. Norton & Co., 2015, pp. 597–605. Disillusioned by the lack of reform within Hinduism, he became a Buddhist in 1956, together with about 200,000 fellow Dalits, at a public ceremony in Nagpur.

30 Rambachan, *A Hindu Theology of Liberation*, p. 177.

31 Rambachan, *A Hindu Theology of Liberation*, p. 177.

32 *Laudato Si'*, § 238–40, Pope Francis' reflection on the Trinity, creation and the universe.

33 Rambachan, *A Hindu Theology of Liberation*, pp. 102–3.

34 Rambachan, *A Hindu Theology of Liberation*, p. 104.

35 *Bhagavad Gita* 13.27.

36 Raimon Panikkar, *Obras Completas VIII Visión trinitaria y cosmoteándrica: Dios-Hombre-Cosmos*, I: La Divinidad, Barcelona: Herder Editorial, 2016, pp. 27–63, at p. 29; cf. B. Kumarappa, *The Hindu Conception of the Deity as Culminating in Ramanuja*, London: Luzac & Co, 1934.

37 Apostolic Journey of His Holiness Pope Francis to the United Arab Emirates, 3–5 February 2019, Interreligious Meeting, Address of His Holiness, Founder's Memorial (Abu Dhabi), Monday, 4 February 2019, Vatican City: Libreria Editrice Vaticana.

38 Pope Francis, cited from the 'Interregious General Audience on the Occasion of the 50th Anniversary of the Promulgation of the Conciliar Declaration "Nostra Aetate"', St Peter's Square, Wednesday, 28 October 2015, Vatican City: Libreria Editrice Vaticana, cf. *Nostra Aetate* § 5.

39 'Introduction' to *A Document on Human Fraternity for World Peace and Living Together*, Abu Dhabi, 4 February 2019, Vatican City: Libreria Editrice Vaticana.

40 'Introduction' to *A Document on Human Fraternity for World Peace and Living Together*.

41 'Introduction' to *A Document on Human Fraternity for World Peace and Living Together*.

42 'Introduction' to *A Document on Human Fraternity for World Peace and Living Together*.

43 *A Document on Human Fraternity for World Peace and Living Together*.

44 The meeting took place at HE's office at the Ministry on Sunday, 18 June 2017.

45 Angeliki Ziaka, 'Introduction' to Shaikh Abdullah bin Mohammed Al Salmi, *Religious Tolerance: A Vision for a New World*, ed. Angeliki Ziaka, Hildesheim, Zürich and New York: Georg Olms Verlag, 2016.

46 Dr F. A. Nizami, 'Introduction' to HE Sheikh Abdullah bin Mohammed al Salmi, *Belief and Righteous Work: An Open Vision for a New World*. Oxford: Oxford Centre for Islamic Studies, 2012, pp. 5–7 at p. 6.

47 Any recognized group needs to register at the Ministry of Endowments and Religious Affairs.

48 As a recognition in 2010, Sultan Qaboos awarded HE *Alrusoukh* (Firmness) Medal Grade I. In 2012, the Queen of the Netherlands awarded him the Order of the Kingdom of the Netherlands, and in 2002 the President of Egypt Arab Republic awarded him a medal of Science and Literature; see Angeliki Ziaka, 'Introduction', p. 156.

49 Shaikh Abdullah bin Mohammed Al Salmi, 'The Influence of Religion on Strategic Decision-Making: Some Reflections on the Present Day Situation' – speech at the National Defense College, Muscat, 24 October 2013. Seven speeches are published in Al Salmi, *Religious Tolerance*.

50 Al Salmi, 'The Influence of Religion on Strategic Decision-Making', p. 244.

51 Al Salmi, 'The Influence of Religion on Strategic Decision-Making', p. 244.

52 Al Salmi, *Belief and Righteous Work*, p. 11.

53 Al Salmi, *Belief and Righteous Work*, p. 12.

54 Al Salmi, *Belief and Righteous Work*, p. 13.

55 Al Salmi, *Belief and Righteous Work*, p. 15.

56 'Conflict of Hegemony and the Discord in Relationships', Al Salmi, *Belief and Righteous Work*, pp. 15–25 at p. 16.

57 Regarding numbers, it is plausible to suggest that Hinduism has also provided large numbers and influences, but Hinduism, having been absent from Europe at the beginnings of modernity, was colonially excluded from its effect on many millions of people. The same stands for Buddhism in all its forms.

58 HE relies here on the work of the historian Toby Huff; see *Intellectual Curiosity and the Scientific Revolution: A Global Perspective*, Cambridge: Cambridge University Press, 2011; and *The Rise of Early Modern Science: Islam, China and the West*, 3rd and updated edn, Cambridge: Cambridge University Press, 2017.

59 Scholars of colonialism, such as Valentin Mudimbe and those Christian theologians of inculturation such as Aylward Shorter, would agree with HE in that within the expansion of Christianity cultural traits of European and Roman thought prevailed over the gospel, so that the Christianity that was encountered after the sixteenth century was a colonial construct of oppression rather than a Christianity that reflected the gospel values of freedom.

60 Al Salmi, *Belief and Righteous Work*, pp. 24–5.

61 Al Salmi, *Belief and Righteous Work*, p. 26.

62 Al Salmi, *Belief and Righteous Work*, p. 27.

63 Al Salmi, *Belief and Righteous Work*, p. 28.

64 Al Salmi, *Belief and Righteous Work*, p. 29.

65 Al Salmi, *Belief and Righteous Work*, p. 29.

66 Al Salmi, *Belief and Righteous Work*, p. 31.

67 Al Salmi, *Belief and Righteous Work*, pp. 32–3.

68 Al Salmi, *Belief and Righteous Work*, pp. 33–4.

69 Al Salmi, *Belief and Righteous Work*, pp. 34–5.

70 Al Salmi, *Belief and Righteous Work*, pp. 35–6.

71 '50th Anniversary Celebration of the Pontifical Council for Interreligious Dialogue: Welcome of Cardinal Jean-Louis Tauran', 19 May 2014, The Vatican, at www.pcinterreligious.org/jeanlouis-tauran-en-2014, accessed 31.8.20.

4

Interfaith Dialogue, the Indigenous, and Liberating Praxis

This chapter explores the common purpose of liberation and dialogue, praxis and orthodoxy, in the past years and during the pandemic. It looks at the cooperation between the different faith communities to help neighbours and others, again with an emphasis on the presence of faith outside Europe and North America. It is here that during the pandemic good will between faith communities started returning to the basics of each world religion, based on the respect for life, the presence of the Divine in the world, and the compassion and solidarity that many times had been forgotten. Liberating praxis that was a challenge to Christian theology in the 1960s and 1970s within a majority Christian continent such as Latin America becomes the centre for a 'universal responsibility' of liberating others from poverty and oppression. However, it becomes a common liberating theological project for practitioners of different religions together. Such praxis, liberation and dialogue is not confined any longer to Christianity in the sense of ecumenism, or to world religions in the manner of interreligious dialogue, but expands to localized understandings of creation, life and eschatology that were there before the arrival of powerful narratives of world religions and the understanding of the Divine as the One and the Only One. It is through a fresh reading of the context of Gutiérrez and Casaldáliga that I will argue that they were involved not only in a liberating praxis but also in an intense cultural dialogue as interreligious dialogue, a path that must be strengthened.

Liberating Praxis and Historical Structural Sins

The globalization of the planet and of the markets has triggered a dichotomy between a connected world that appears in the media and a world that independently operates in an indigenous way, usually within the socio-political peripheries of postcolonial elites. For example, Amazonia in Latin America, Brazil as a state portrays an image of progress that resembles Portuguese colonial times. Brazil remains a world economic power but the power of Evangelicals, Pentecostals and born-again Christians has changed the political face of a country that associates economic progress with a gospel of prosperity and divine rewards. This has been a change from the times in which the Brazilian bishops and cardinals were deemed to be the most progressive and powerful within the Catholic Church. Is this just a change of Christian tradition within the elites of Brazil? I am not interested here in a sociological analysis but in the possibilities of a liberating praxis that could serve and learn from the poor and the marginalized. Such liberating praxis of a gospel associated with the poor and the marginalized has changed within the corridors of power and the figure of President Bolsonaro has expressed it very clearly: Brazil is a sovereign state and therefore international outcries about the burning of the Amazonia are not allowed. International aid to control the fires was not permitted either, and the confrontation between landowners backed by the government and indigenous populations was only delayed by the pandemic. I return to some basics of liberation theology based on the gospel and the values of the Kingdom of God: the central value of the gospel is not private property, but subsidiarity from God and solidarity with others. God is the Lord of history and therefore all possessions are a gift from God. The land belongs to God and we are only stewards of this planet. Further, within international treaties, Amazonia is recognized as a world's patrimony as in the case of Antarctica and other natural reserves of our planet.

I would argue here that ecological discourses and the care of creation are not fashionable discourses but themes of orthopraxis that were diluted by colonial powers and reshaped within postcolonial discourses of universal values and global subsidiarity. Structural sin, either in Amazonia or in the case of the Dalit of India, or within the ethnic minorities of Africa, has been a challenge to social and political structures that by the action of human beings have created social injustices. Thus, in the case of Amazonia and at Puebla de los Angeles in 1979, Pope John Paul II warned against a political praxis when he addressed the bishops of Latin America, stating that 'they were responsible for their flock and for the community as such'. Indeed, I have chosen to reread the reflection by the very traditional Cardinal Alfonso López Trujillo 25 years after the conference at Puebla, because even that reflection adheres to the care for social justice and progress as outlined by Paul VI's *Populorum Progressio* (1967).[1] Within such a seminal document for Christianity and development in Latin America, Paul VI outlined very clearly a summary of the responsibility of the rich towards the poor as a sign of the love of God (1 John 3.17).[2] Further, Pope Francis worked theologically through the tradition by citing St Ambrose:

> You are not making a gift of what is yours to the poor man, but you are giving him back what is his. You have been appropriating things that are meant to be for the common use of everyone. The earth belongs to everyone, not to the rich.[3]

In the conclusion to *Populorom Progressio*, Paul VI stated that 'the right to private property is not absolute and unconditional'.[4] The common good becomes a primary social situation and therefore 'no one may appropriate surplus goods solely for his own private use when others lack the bare necessities of life'.[5]

Amazonia: An Interreligious Theology of the Poor

Years of struggle for justice and inclusion have focused on Amazonia because of its importance for several countries, the large number of indigenous populations attached to Amazonia, and the global interest in its ecosystems, fauna, flora and the river itself.[6] Indeed, Amazonia has been a geopolitical challenge since colonial times and the arrival of the Spanish and the Portuguese. The hope of a full integration of diverse indigenous peoples within independent nations was never realized. By the 1960s, and Vatican II, questioning about their mutual roles was expressed by the Amazonian peoples, the Catholic Church, anthropologists, scientists and the states involved, Brazil being the largest among them.

Gutiérrez moved to a rereading of Latin American history by assuming God's involvement in human history throughout the Hebrew Scriptures. For him, the history of Latin America was no different from that of Israel, because within that human history there were God-fearing people who asked questions about history in order to understand questions about God. If the liberation of Israel through the Exodus made a people, Gutiérrez explored the 'encounter' between Europeans and indigenous peoples in 1492. Christians led a colonial conquest based initially on ideals of civilization and evangelization, but that was subsequently driven by human greed and an ongoing strife for riches and power.[7] Those who suffered poverty and social annihilation under the conquistadors became part of a society that proclaimed itself Christian, and in the name of an unjust Christian relation between colonizers and colonized subjected indigenous peoples to slavery, genocide, forced conversion and inhuman conditions of life.[8] Nevertheless, for Gutiérrez, God was in Latin America in pre-Columbian times and he remained with the suffering indigenous peoples while many atrocities were taking place.

In reading Latin American history, Gutiérrez isolated the example of some Christians who did not comply with the status quo of colonialism and degradation, and became themselves defenders of the poor for the sake of the gospel. One of them, Bishop Bartolomé de Las Casas, was an example of a full conversion to the poor in colonial Latin America that allowed their voice to be heard within the Spanish courts and the learned universities of Europe.[9] Las Casas' Christian attitude made a difference in God's action in history because he defended the poor and the needy, and in return he became a sign of contradiction that had to suffer attacks from philosophers, theologians and conquistadors alike.[10] Those attacks came upon him because Las Casas not only exercised Christian charity towards the indigenous populations but constructed a theologically informed defence of their human rights because of their condition as children of God made in God's own image.[11]

In his defence of the indigenous populations Las Casas resembled Job, another biblical figure important for Gutiérrez. If Gutiérrez dwells on the suffering of the innocent by examining the book of Job he does so by associating the person of Job not with a passive sufferer but with an example of suffering-trust in God and his love for all.[12] Job in the Bible and Bartolomé de Las Casas in the Latin American context become prototypes of Christian history because they are able not only to empathize with those suffering but because in enduring physical and emotional suffering themselves they do not see God through a general depersonalized historical narrative but see the poor as protagonists of that history. Thus, they develop a theology that speaks once and again of the love of God in a human history in need of liberation and not in a theology ridden with clauses, argumentations and intellectual discourses attached to the learned and to philosophers.

Bartolomé welds faith to what we today would call social analysis. This enables him to unmask the 'social sin' of his time. That, doubtless, was his forte – and also the difference between him and the great majority of those in Spain who were concerned with the affairs of the Indies. Those who had not seen the abuse and contempt to which the Indians were subjected, those who had not suffered in their own flesh the aggression of the mighty ones of the Indies, those who had not counted dead bodies, had other priorities in theology.[13]

During this period of biblical and theological reflection

Gutiérrez brings together the concept of the God of history, already present in his *A Theology of Liberation*, with a shift in Latin American ecclesial history towards the place where the God of history makes his presence felt: the world of the poor. The 'irruption of the poor' within Latin America suggests that the centrality of the poor within the practice of religion should bring a change in the political understanding of social, economic and power relations. If the Christian communities of Latin America, and therefore the Latin American Church, decided to strive for the world of the poor because it was among the poor that the incarnate Son of God decided to dwell, the political world should do the same, particularly in a continent where most politicians have declared themselves Christians and are part of that servant Church of the poor. The 'preferential option for the poor' forwarded by Gutiérrez and others, and sanctioned within the pastoral options of the Latin American Church, constitutes not just a change in pastoral orientation but 'is nothing short of a Copernican revolution for the Church'.[14]

Gutiérrez explores God's involvement in human history through the religious practice of his Church in the past, but in doing so he moves with theological, religious and political questions that arise in present-day Latin America. The publication of *A Theology of Liberation* takes place after the implementation of Vatican II in Latin America, through the second meeting of all Latin American Bishops in Medellin (Colombia), while Gutiérrez' second period of theological reflection coincides with the third meeting of Latin American Bishops in Puebla de Los Angeles (Mexico) in 1979. It is at Puebla that the 'preferential option for the poor' is publicly declared by the meeting of bishops within the political climate of a number of military coups, including those in Chile (1973) and Argentina (1976), while the force of Medellin remains the crucial impact for Gutiérrez' theology. It is at Medellin in 1968 that the theological movement of a Latin America driven by lay unpublished theologians began.[15] The Church in Latin America had to ask questions about their religious practice within difficult political circumstances, and aided by the theological reflection of

Gutiérrez the bishops did not separate religion and politics, but provided a political response of commitment to political change and the defence of human rights. However, the subsequent pastoral implementation of Medellin was varied, so that in the case of Chile the bishops challenged the military regime but there was an avoidance of any prophetic denunciation in the case of Argentina.[16]

Gutiérrez provides a clear biblical and theological reflection that does not differentiate between religion and politics, because those processes are neither separated in the Hebrew Scriptures nor in the history of the Church in Latin America. The politics of religion that a local church decides to implement cannot be influenced by theology as a second step, but must reflect the first step of commitment and practice – with the poor in the case of Gutiérrez, with the wealthy and powerful in the case of many clergymen and bishops of Latin America. For, Gutiérrez' return to the biblical sources follows from his own commitment to the poor, his own involvement with the reading of contemporary history in Latin America, and his own involvement with important ecclesiastical figures such as Helder Camara, Pedro Casaldáliga, Oscar Romero, Evaristo Arns and Manuel Larraín.

A Spirituality of Liberation

During a third period of action, reflection and writing, Gutiérrez asked questions about the response to God's actions in history by the Latin American poor and marginalized. The poor also do theology because they reflect on the Scriptures together, allowing for narratives on the action of God in the world to be articulated. Their religious response through their Christian life produces different localized ways of responding to the work of the Holy Spirit, thus producing new spiritualities.

Spirituality for Gutiérrez does not relate to a pious individual response to God in order to acquire security; on the contrary, an honest response to God creates insecurity, persecution, misunderstanding and suffering. The actions of those who respond to the Holy Spirit do not always please the powerful and the rich; thus the poor become ever more dependent on God, not on their own means. Religion as a way of life based on the Spirit produces men and women who trust and wait for God's promises while sharing solidarity with the poor and the marginalized within communities. Thus, Gutiérrez challenges the idea of a self-sufficient individualistic spirituality that creates prosperity and security. On the contrary, he systematizes the possibility of a distinct Latin American spirituality closer to the values of the Kingdom and far from the security of riches, power and social acceptance.[17]

Spirituality, for Gutiérrez, is a way of life that moves towards the poor because the poor are the ones who show more trust and need of God, not because they are better than other human beings. Spirituality becomes a method for theology because a way of life close to the poor comes before any theological thinking or writing. Thus, religion as a practice informs the involvement of Christians within politics because all actions that precede theology are enacted within society, within the *polis*, and therefore they are all political. Even those who practise a spirituality that agrees with the status quo express opinions within society, and therefore within the realm of political governance; they elect politicians, professional governors, according to their beliefs, according to their spirituality, according to their theology, according to their preferences that rationally cannot be contrary to their way of life.

For Gutiérrez, God is at the centre of that social and religious change that allows human beings to be liberated from their own personal sin, but most importantly from sinful structures that do not allow them to be fully human and in God's image. Thus, in his later work, Gutiérrez, who so far has not allowed for a separation between religion and politics, returns to the theme of liberation by returning to reflections on the action of God as liberator in the Bible, within a particular history. God is the God of life because he liberates. However, Gutiérrez makes very clear distinctions about the fact that God is a liberator when he writes:

God is not a liberator because God liberates; rather God liberates because God is a liberator. God is not just because he establishes justice, or faithful because God enters into a covenant, but the other way around. I am not playing with words here, but trying to bring out the primacy and transcendence of God and to remind ourselves that God's being gives meaning to God's action. According to the Bible, God's interventions in the life of God's people do not imply any kind of immanentism or any dissolution of God into history; rather they emphasize that God is the absolute and transcendent sort of being.[18]

In this late reflection on God and his work, Gutiérrez synthesizes his theology by integrating the Latin American context and the action of the absolute being that is much preferred within European discourses on transcendence and immanence. The difference in his discourse in relation to other theologians is that any discourse about God arises out of a communal practice of social justice within the *polis* and not in isolation from those social realities. For Gutiérrez is not making an attempt to integrate two separate realities, that is, religion and politics; the separation is in the mind, while the practice indicates that theological discourses and the act of contemplation constitute a political act of prophetic solidarity, defiance and social pronouncement. It is at the end of his theological book on God that Gutiérrez discloses the possibility of a relation between aesthetics, poetics and God's option for the poor, by outlining the hope that comes out of suffering in the poetic works of César Vallejo.[19] He does not return to theological aesthetics and instead continues an exploration of history within a Latin American postmodernity.

Gutiérrez' later theological work, always a reflection on his pastoral work, is influenced by the preparations for the five-hundredth anniversary of the encounter between indigenous peoples and Europeans. As the Latin American Church prepared for the Fourth General Meeting of Latin American Bishops in Santo Domingo, Gutiérrez, as a theological expert, realized that, for some, 1492 meant a great moment of discovery, for others a great moment of evangelization, but for the indigenous peoples of Latin America it meant an encounter with a colonial machine that destroyed, enslaved and did not differentiate the religion and politics of empire. While historians such as Enrique Dussel explored the chronological periods and changes of the Church in Latin America, Gutiérrez delivered an uncompromizing Christian manifesto of solidarity with the indigenous peoples of Latin America, but within the context of the Church.

The context of the Latin American Church at Santo Domingo was already postmodern and post-romantic. The military regimes in Latin America had ceased to exist, civil wars in Guatemala and El Salvador were coming to an end, and the influence of a neo-liberal economic system that fostered individualism, economic prosperity and personal salvation was felt throughout the continent. The rise of Protestantism pointed to a refreshed Christianity for Latin America but in many cases the individual salvation supported by those Christian groups coming from North America undermined the pastoral aims and objectives of the Christian communities. The violence of the military regimes had ended but the violent protests by indigenous peoples against the state had brought new challenges associated with indigenous rights, international laws of cultural protection, and the recovery of indigenous sacred landscapes and political spaces.

Gutiérrez took active part in the 1992 meeting of bishops in Santo Domingo and together with others he challenged the neo-conservatism coming out of the Vatican and of the newly appointed bishops, most of them of a more neo-scholastic way of thinking. If for some of them religion and politics could be separated, Gutiérrez returned in his theological writings to the social doctrine of the Church and to the pastoral achievements of Medellin and Puebla. If Vatican II had prepared the way for a clear engagement of the Church with the contemporary world, it was the reflection on ecclesial praxis at Medellin and Puebla that had provided the theory and method for being religious in Latin America. The epistemology of Medellin, particularly, had indicated that it was not possible to do theology without a commitment to the poor and that to be committed to the poor a religious practitioner had to engage with the political in order to influence it for the sake of the poor. Thus, democratic or non-democratic institutions did not perceive the poor as the recipients of good news but as a social and political problem. Economic growth and successful economic policies did not take into account the human value of the poor but were geared to maximize profit in order to implement successful economic models of development that benefited few and punished the majority that did not have resources for economic growth or investment.

For Gutiérrez, the newly centred reflections on the religious, the social and the political stem from the centrality of the human person. Political systems that are not person-centred fail to understand the beauty of God's creation of man and woman in his own image. For example, on the subject of work and coinciding with John Paul II's encyclical letter *Laborem Exercens*, Gutiérrez argues that the dignity of the person who works comes from the fact that a human being is recreating the earth, and not from the type of work undertaken, a clear break from the Spanish colonial understanding that there was a higher type of work, a more intellectual one, that left a lower type of manual work to slaves and servants.[20] However, Gutiérrez recognizes that for some commentators the Pope seems to be speaking about the third world only, and that is not the case. The encyclical recalls the dignity of every human being everywhere and the absolute primacy of the human over technological discoveries, economic and political systems that place profit over workers and economic growth over human dignity. As already argued at Medellin, the call of the Church is to denounce poverty but also to show through material poverty that human beings remain at the centre of passing systems, policies and social structures, be they just or unjust. Thus, Gutiérrez argues forcefully:

The encyclical clearly describes the universality of the social problem, the depth of the injustice and the abandonment suffered by the poor today, the responsibility of leaders of socio-economic systems which violate the rights of workers, and the urgent need for the whole Church to make the cause of the dispossessed her own.[21]

To be religious within that society that violates human dignity and favours markets over people requires a return to the body of social teaching of the Church, not to foster solely academic study but in order to give further authority to the already plentiful commitment by Christian communities towards the poor. It requires a return to the idea articulated by the Church Fathers that a Christian life needs a style of life that visibly speaks of the religious. Therefore, words and confessions do not match a style of life in solidarity with the poor, in which what is given is not only the excess gained but the goods acquired by human and divine right. A style of life and a spirituality of poverty do not become an exception to ordinary life but the norm of the life of all Christians and of the Church. Thus, Gregory the Great wrote:

> The earth is common to all men, and therefore the food it provides is produced by all in common. Thus, they are wrong to believe themselves innocent who demand for their private use the gift that God gave to all ... when we give what is indispensable to the needy, we do not do them a favour from our personal generosity, but we return to them what is theirs. More than an act of charity, what we are doing is fulfilling an obligation of justice.[22]

It is that theology of daily life, of a style of life, of a social morality of connection with other human beings, that makes Gutiérrez' theological agenda meaningful as well as central within a post-socialist world. Those who understood his agenda as a religious commitment to socialist ideas rather than to Christian ideas saw an end to liberation theology after the collapse of socialist states in Eastern Europe during the 1990s. However, the religious preoccupation with the poor and the oppressed can only end when there is no more poverty. Until then the voice of the poor in theology, in the practice of religion and in politics is to be heard as a central commitment to the building of the Kingdom of God now and for the future. The Church as the body of believers and as a signifier of God's presence altered the role of the poor at Medellin, where they became theological and political actors in society. The task remains, according to Jon Sobrino, to make the Church of the poor a reality in order to continue challenging the centrality of wealth and profit in the running of society.[23] Sobrino, as well as Gutiérrez, points to the fact that the Christian utopia of religion and politics has not been realized; however, both of them remain committed to bridge any separation between religious practice and governance, between the world of the poor and the neo-liberal world that dominated Latin America at the beginning of the twenty-first century.[24]

Theological Solidarity

As already argued, within Gutiérrez' writings there is no clear separation between the religious and the political. Theological narratives about God textually re-create understandings of a divine history that is expressed through human history, following Nicholas Lash's theological dictum: 'All human utterances occur in a context. And the contexts in which they occur modify their meaning.'[25] Thus, Gutiérrez provides a challenge to any privatization of theological reflection concentrated in academia, but he also assumes that a few within the theological community and the Christian community exercise their Christian mission within universities and theological colleges through an ongoing ministry of teaching and research.

For Gutiérrez, the relation between the practice of religion and the practice of politics needs to be articulated through the Christian faith. Within that relation, commitment to the poor and the marginalized in the name of God provides the first step of involvement by Christians in the world, and particularly within the social context of Latin America. That commitment to justice and to the poor is the first step in any theological reflection about the world and its relation to God. Faith comes first, and reason follows because 'theology is an understanding of the faith. It is a rereading of the word of God as that word is lived in the Christian community', so that 'we can separate theological reflection neither from the Christian community nor from the world in which that community lives'.[26]

Gutiérrez' reflection on the relation between religion and politics presupposes an ongoing commitment to God through the poor of society that is inscribed much later in theological narratives about the love of God for human beings and the need for the theologian to immerse herself in that extension of the incarnation in contemporary human history. Thus, her theologizing differs from political theology, theologies of development and theologies of revolution because in all those theological movements the articulation of ideas and writings comes first, the practice of religion and politics comes second. What unites all those theological models is a Christian response to individualistic models related to romantic movements, post-Enlightenment ideas and the postmodern condition.

Religion as the practice of faith becomes politics because Christians involve themselves in their own contexts in solidarity with the poor and the marginalized. If the response to modernity had been to reject the world and to establish immanent truths with the help of reason and philosophy, Gutiérrez provides continuity to Bonhoeffer's theological commitment by assuming that at the root of a Christian response to modernity is the search for a life in Christ that is lived 'irreligiously' by expressing solidarity with others.[27] For Bonhoeffer, to practise religion was to assume the life of the weak and suffering God of the cross; for Gutiérrez, to practise religion is to assume the politics of the weak and the suffering human beings who represent the face of God.[28] Thus, solidarity with the oppressed presumes a critique of the political establishment that in most cases has failed to protect the poor and of Christians who had failed to practise the ethical values of religion within the social spheres of political influence. If initially Gutiérrez could have followed some of the Latin American theologians calling for a socialist-oriented society, his methodological critique of the possibility of a single political model and a continuous solidarity with the poor would have made Gutiérrez' forceful assessment of the religious and the political even more important in understanding the involvement of Christians within the contemporary world in a post-Soviet Union and post-9/11 world.[29] In the words of Gutiérrez:

> We shall not have our great leap forward, into a whole new theological perspective, until the marginalized and exploited have begun to become the artisans of their own liberation – until their voice makes itself heard directly, without mediation, without interpreters – until they themselves take account, in the light of their own values, of their own experience of the Lord in their efforts to liberate themselves. We shall not have our quantum theological leap until the oppressed themselves theologise, until 'the others' themselves personally reflect on their hope of a total liberation in Christ. For they are the bearers of this hope for all humanity.[30]

The conclusion is simple: the sole practice and advancement of theology depends on the right relation between religion and politics; thus, the theological project is to be realized as a second act of solidarity rather than as the only possible intellectual response to human solidarity – and therefore becoming a selfish individual act. Thus, 'in searching for this meaning, the theologian knows that, as Clodovis Boff says, everything is politics but politics is not everything'.[31]

I would argue that it is within Amazonia that we have not only one of the first ecclesial struggles for social justice after Vatican II but it is also where we can experience the theological link between a developed sense of 'our common home' and at the same time the interfaith dialogue for social justice that integrates indigenous traditions into the concept of interreligious dialogue. It is in Amazonia that the struggles for liberation and the advancement of a metaphysical dialogue of different worlds take place, making liberation theology and interreligious dialogue a common path and a common place for Christianity and theologizing by the poor and marginalized. *Nostra Aetate* did not go far enough in Vatican II, and documents such as

Evangelium Nuntiandi, Medellin and Puebla had not managed to grasp the importance of Amazonia for theologies of liberation and interreligious dialogue. It was in the conference of the Latin American bishops at Santo Domingo (1992), in the context of the five-hundredth anniversary of the encounter between indigenous populations and Europeans, that reflections could be explored on the importance of the indigenous populations for the development of the Kingdom of God.

Within such an advance in intra-religious dialogue with the poor and marginalized of colonialism and of the modern state, the conference at Aparecida settled the relation between indigenous communities and the gospel not as utilitarian but as cooperative in respect and dialogue. Such a foundation was carried forward by the head of the redaction team at Aparecida, Archbishop Jorge Bergoglio, who in 2013 became Pope Francis. His visit to Amazonia and its fostering of a clearer understanding of the centrality of Amazonia for the Church and for the world was channelled by the Amazonian Synod held in Rome (6–27 October 2019), and the publication of the Post Synodal Apostolic Exhortation *Querida Amazonia,* given in Rome on 2 February 2020.

The start of such a very strong theological drive towards dialogue with the Amazonian peoples can be traced to the life of Bishop Pedro Casaldáliga, who died in August 2020 just as the recommendations of *Querida Amazonia* were being implemented. Casaldáliga represented continuity because he served as a bishop of the Catholic Church throughout the whole formative period of liberation theology and at the same time retired just as new globalized works on the environment, Amazonia and the warming of the planet became central not only to theology but also to the governments of the powerful nations as well. Casaldáliga brings a freshness of the periphery to Latin American theology; he remained in his rural Amazonian diocese, in the contemplation of God and his creation, writing poetry and enjoying the journey with his people. If Latin American theologians seem angry commentators on social realities, Casaldáliga brings spirituality and the joy of conversation with God into theology so that theology as faith seeking understanding arises out of spirituality – in the case of Casaldáliga, out of a spirituality of liberation.

The Brazilian Context

Brazil was the first Latin American country to push the formation of the Basic Christian Communities, the reading of the Bible at all levels and the involvement of the Catholic Church within the ongoing social realities of ordinary people; however, the 1964 military coup focused most of the Church's attention on a repressive situation rather than on a creative one. It is difficult to know, for example, if the Brazilian Church would have grown so much after Vatican II and Medellin without that experience of a military dictatorship, but certainly Brazilian Catholics were more active in socio-political life than those of Argentina or Chile at the time of Vatican II and therefore at the time of the military coup.[32]

In March 1964 a military coup, supported by civilian conspirators, deposed President João Goulart and started an authoritarian system of government under which the president was designated by the army and approved by the Brazilian congress.[33] The system, with periodical moves from mild liberalism to further authoritarianism, was to last until 1985, when the first attempts to pass legislation that allowed the direct election of the Brazilian president and the control of the budget were restored to the national congress.[34] Therefore, the most seminal years of Boff's theological output took place while the Brazilian state was arresting and torturing dissenters and within a continuous political game of considerable violence between the police, the guerrillas and some right-wing paramilitary groups. Brazilian security and interrogation advisors were provided to other emerging military regimes, such as the Chilean military in 1973, and Brazil also supported the work of the Southern Cone intelligence forces through *Operación Cóndor*.[35]

Casaldáliga was part of a very active Catholic Church with prominent personalities such as Cardinal Evaristo Arns (São Paulo) and Archbishop Helder Cámara (Recife and Olinda), and he became part of a revered generation of Brazilian bishops.[36] The Brazilian Basic Christian Communities united in a large movement, known as the 'popular movement', and asked questions not only about social, economic and political participation in Brazil but also about the democratization of the Catholic Church and the creation of a 'popular Church'.[37] Within those challenges, large sectors of the Brazilian Church's hierarchy became active in politics and, as it was to be in the Chilean case, the Catholic Church in Brazil became part of the few voices of dissent towards subsequent authoritarian regimes.[38] Thus, over a period of 30 years from the formation of the National Bishops' Conference of Brazil (CNBB) in October 1952, the Catholic Church changed its view of the world and chose to be politically involved in the name of the gospel.[39]

With the end of the military regimes, the Basic Christian Communities became involved in national movements that supported the landless, the problems of recuperation of the Amazonian forest, and the preservation of ecological areas threatened by multinational corporations and their enormous overexploitation of natural resources that had previously been privatized and sold to multinational companies by the military. Casaldáliga was part of that ecological crisis because he lived in a diocese that was part of the Brazilian Amazonian basin and his pastoral concerns involved the daily lives of the indigenous community vis-à-vis growing urban centres that resembled colonial enclaves of transient populations and forgotten worlds. Casaldáliga's preoccupation with Latin America came out of his own involvement with the world of the Amazon, and over the 2000 jubilee year the Amazon became part of the preoccupation of a universal humanity concerned not about others' welfare but with its own survival as a species. In the words of Casaldáliga, 'the inventory of iniquity' by transnational corporations includes the destruction of the Amazonian forest:

'The beautiful mother Earth', as Francis of Assisi would say, is being brutally violated. Its products are no longer natural, they are transgenic. And just in our Brazil, in only one year,

16,838 square kilometres were deforested. And in Amazonia the equivalent of seven thousand football fields of trees are cut down every day. One fourth of the surface of the land is under the threat of becoming a desert.[40]

Those concerns, social, religious and political, shaped the life of the young Claretian priest who arrived in Brazil at a time when a new world and a new society were being shaped not only by the conflicts of the Cold War but by the hopes of a new socialist utopia throughout Latin America and within the Catholic Church.

An Amazonian Bishop

Pedro Casaldáliga was born in Balsareny, Catalonia, Spain, in 1928, the son of a farm worker. He was ordained as a priest in Montjuich, Barcelona, on 31 May 1952. A member of the Claretians, he served as Catholic bishop of the diocese of São Félix do Araguaia, Brazil, from 1971 to 2004.[41]

Why Brazil? At the Claretian congregation general chapter of 1967, members of that religious congregation evaluated their own response to the recently concluded Second Vatican Council. As a result, Casaldáliga was given the option of going overseas, either to Bolivia or Brazil. Following the advice of the Claretian Superior General, Peter Schweiger, he opted for Brazil and on 28 January 1968 arrived there, the year in which the Latin American bishops met at Medellin (Colombia) and the Institutional Act (A15) cemented the military regime in Brazil. In July 1968 he arrived in São Félix do Araguaia during one of the strongest periods of political repression, and over the years he helped to start a Pastoral Commission for Land (Comissão Pastoral da Terra CPT) and an indigenous missionary council (Conselho Indigenista Missionário – CIMI) within a territory in which social conflicts over land are usual and quite violent.[42] His diocese, located within the Brazilian state of Mato Grosso, was the size of Catalonia, with 120,000 people living in the territory.

There is no doubt that Casaldáliga loved his pastoral work in Brazil; he became a Brazilian not by birth or adoption but by social upbringing.[43] Casaldáliga, the poet, addressed many poems, songs and letters to Brazil, as a diverse group of people, as a fervent mass of dancing human beings who live in noise and in community. Towards the end of his service as a bishop, for example, Casaldáliga wrote:

> You, Brazil, have a clear call to give a lead; not, of course, in the sense of being a leading power, but of leading in service in solidarity, of setting a coherent example, of providing brotherly encouragement, in our America most specifically but also to a certain extent in relationship with other countries of the so-called Third World, especially with certain African peoples (from whom you also derive and to whom you should return in solidarity). To do so, your first task is clearly to become more Latin American yourself. You often feel yourself to be somehow set apart, like a sort of autonomous continent. Never forget that you are America, my Brazil – Latin America, Amerindia, Afro-America, and our America![44]

His first pastoral letter, dated 23 October 1971, provided a full evaluation of the social conflicts within his diocese and included a call to all to increase their Christian commitment to the gospel through justice and peace work in the context of the private ownership of land and social conflict vis-à-vis the need for agrarian reform.[45] Throughout his episcopal life he lived very simply in a house that resembled every other house, usually open to the passer-by and to the people around him. In 1976 he survived a serious attempt on his life when the bullet aimed at him killed the Jesuit priest João Bosco Burnier who was beside him. That incident was to mark the life of his diocese, and yearly a diocesan pilgrimage departed to the place where Burnier had been killed, a place that became a place of memory, martyrdom and devotion for all the victims of political violence within the diocese.[46] In his own assessment, Casaldáliga recognized that the difficulties between him and the local government were a product of the fact that he lived close to the territory where the guerrillas of Araguaia operated. The Brazilian army, air force, navy and police carried out four major war operations against the guerrillas by surrounding the territory occupied by Casaldáliga's prelature and by arresting people, some of whom were tortured. Many of them were members of the Basic Christian Communities, and Casaldáliga denounced the military operation. As a result, the Brazilian government tried to expel him from the country five times. However, Pope Paul VI was very clear on this matter and told Mgr Paulo Evaristo Arns to let the Brazilian government know that any hostile act against Casaldáliga would be considered an attack on the Pope and the Vatican (whoever attacks Peter also attacks Paul). Casaldáliga did not have to leave the country but he was kept under house arrest.

After the military regime ended in Brazil, Casaldáliga had to deal with the land owners and the increased privatization of lands, a product of the free market economy embraced by Brazil. There were many warnings that if he continued interfering something very serious could happen to him. It never did, in the words of Casaldáliga, 'because his hour had not come and God wanted him to mature as a human being'.[47]

In 2003 he sent his letter of resignation to the Pope, as expected of all Catholic bishops who reach the age of 75, having been diagnosed with Parkinson's disease and high blood pressure.[48] His episcopal succession was made conditional on his settlement as bishop emeritus outside his diocese, in order not to interfere with the new bishop who was to be appointed, a fact that was challenged by the pastoral council, which also complained about the fact that they didn't have any say in the appointment of a new bishop. At that moment, Casaldáliga's dream would have been to visit Africa and to pray with Africans in solidarity with the rest of the world, but his health did not allow him to go. Nevertheless, he made a conscious decision to remain in Brazil and not to return to his native Catalonia.

The episcopal succession was a difficult moment for all because the general suspicion, aided by the contemporary experience of the appointment of traditional bishops all over Latin

America, was that John Paul II would appoint somebody with a very different idea of the pastoral priorities and engagement of the Church with contemporary society. After many letters, challenges and misunderstandings, John Paul II appointed a Franciscan friar, Leonardo Ulrich Steiner, as the new bishop of São Félix do Araguaia. Casaldáliga called the new bishop 'a true Franciscan, fraternal, open to dialogue, interested in the people', and that settled the matter.[49] Casaldáliga remained at the banks of the River Araguaia, supporting in his old age the life of those around him until his death in August 2020.

A Passion for Utopia

One of his few public appearances outside his pastoral work (Casaldáliga preferred to pray, to write and to share with the people of his diocese and to remain 'on the red soil') was on 24 October 2000.[50] On that day he was awarded a doctorate *honoris causa* by the State University of Campinas in Brazil.[51] After the award was conferred he gave a lecture that summarized his own life and gratitude to those who worked with him over many years. On that occasion he spoke of his passion for utopia and suggested that passion was the only possible reason for the important university degree awarded to him.

Casaldáliga described himself as out of fashion, in a contemporary world of pragmatisms, productivity, full market economies and postmodernity. His passion, he commented, was always the Kingdom of God, as it was the passion of Christ that coincides with the aspirations of all humanity for a fully human life, an authentic life that is fully happy.[52] The utopia of God and his love is to proclaim a place in this world for all and a place for all in the next world. If only 20 per cent of people have access to the world's commodities and the majority are excluded, Casaldáliga's utopia was to proclaim once again that God wants all to have a place in the universal history that comes out of the here and now. Citing the work of Marciano Vidal on a universal ethics, Casaldáliga pointed to three ethical ways that prepare the Church and every Christian for a new millennium: (1) a pure vision, meaning the possibility of every human being able to appreciate reality without self-interest and without prejudices; (2) a compassionate empathy, meaning an ongoing solidarity with the weak of this world; and (3) a simple lifestyle, in order to create alternative values to those of the contemporary world's complexity. The twenty-first-century manifesto for all, according to Casaldáliga, is the Sermon on the Mount, where those who are blessed are those who follow human attitudes that are very different from the contemporary canon of profit and self-importance, and of a world considered real and tangible in which God and the Kingdom of God does not have a place, a time or social influence.

Casaldáliga, in his acceptance speech at the University of Campinas, proclaimed once again the possibility, not a passive one, of proclaiming hope against all hope, without a religious passivity or a belief in electoral and political promises. Thus, this challenge, he maintained, is not for those who are satisfied with the neo-liberal McDonald's, or those who have packed their flags and gone home defeated. Playing with words and the Brazilian phenomenon of *caminhada*, the walk, and the pilgrimage used to request land and rights by civil society, Casaldáliga assured his audience that the pilgrimage continued and that thousands continued in hope, walking, singing and clapping. That included the university, not at the service of the system but a university at the service of life, at the service of the dispossessed and not the oligarchy, a university that should be pluricultural, political and militant in the defence of the marginalized of society. He proposed to start a new movement of those without university (MSU), because utopias start with a thought and a common consciousness and those thoughts are triggered at the universities. Casaldáliga wanted a utopian university! For Casaldáliga, utopia is dream, is stimulus, is service; we are the road and we are the end of history through the fact that all human beings have a divine gene, a divine DNA that points to humanity rather than profit. The fulfilment of that utopia is not the crucifixion but the resurrection because human beings who live in hope are the resurrection and are the human utopia fulfilled in God's actions.

Casaldáliga's utopian dream of a more just society closer
to the values of the Kingdom of God, and his own aesthetic
sociability and literary life, does not have a hint of escapism.
For his theological narrative of utopianism unveils a certainty
that he associates with the resurrection. 'I believe in the Resurrection,' he proclaims, but he qualifies such optimism with the
following personal assertion: 'Every act of faith in resurrection
has to have a corresponding act of justice, of service, of solidarity, of love.'[53] His utopia remained a clear condemnation of
capitalism as an economic system, and he remained supportive
of the Cuban revolution because, in his own words, 'God never
left Cuba, he remained there.'[54] Socialism could be outdated as
a system vilified by the West, but in Casaldáliga's terms socialism with a utopian sharing and a clear human equality remains
a system closer to gospel values, the values of sharing symbolized by the multiplication of the two loaves and the fish for a
multitude. Those actions are not materialistic actions but they
constitute expressions of a way of life, of a way of encountering God; they remain expressions of a personal and communal
spirituality shared by all Christians. Thus, for a busy bishop
and an extroverted disciple of life and poetry, discussions on
a Latin American spirituality as a way to God became central
to his own pilgrimage as a Christian within the worlds of
Amazonia and of the riverside Araguaia. Casaldáliga was not
only a prophet of liberation but a master of interreligious dialogue in his daily interaction with peoples of the Amazonia and
their different world, their different metaphysics and religious
system but their very similar dreams of utopia and resurrection.

From the Inside to the Outside

Casaldáliga's common attempt with José María Vigil to frame
a spirituality of liberation for the unfinished summa of Latin
American theological works represents the inner need of personal testimony and ascension.[55] For many, Latin American
theology had nothing to do with the spiritual but was concerned with the world of action, and even Gutiérrez' work on a

Latin American spirituality was not given the same prominence as his other work.[56] Even in the case of Ernesto Cardenal, poet and contemplative, the emphasis of the literature was always on the minister and the public figure of the Nicaraguan Sandinistas.[57] However, for Casaldáliga it is the inside of the person, the spiritual self that connects with the outside world and, through utopian moments of self-awareness, challenges the possibility of a non-spiritual world of the material and of matter as the centre of human existence.

Within the history of spirituality – that is, of the different and varied approaches to communication with God and of action within the world – there have been two movements of the human soul signified and represented spatially: from the outside to the inside and vice versa. For the majority of Christians and for the majority of theologians their communication with the God of life takes place within an active life in which movement and human interaction take most of their daily available hours. Prayer opens and closes the day with conversational spells in which humans try to make sense of life and action around them in relation to a third point of the hermeneutical circle: God. As a result, there is a direct connection and relation between religious practitioners of all faiths and all religions. Others instead find the sole of their daily life in the inside of themselves and in an ongoing conversation and contemplation of the Divine. They do not avoid activities and human interaction but their actions and human interactions come out of a spiritual perspective from the inside. Freer than others from material concerns, they relocate God within the spiritual hermeneutical circle to a centre within the human world as a place to which they return from time to time during their daily existence.

Casaldáliga remained a contemplative and an active bishop but he didn't like to travel and his whole pastoral perspective came from within. Firmly rooted within the Amazonia region, he even felt that the visit of all Catholic bishops to Rome in order to report to the Pope (the *ad limina* visit) was not a central point in his life and by association of the life of bishops as they tried to serve God.[58] In a sense, Casaldáliga returned to the colonial time of the Jesuits and their reductions, and remained within a world that integrated the spiritual and the material by centring all causal explanations on the spiritual world. Casaldáliga felt at home within that reality by stressing the importance of the spiritual. He didn't avoid the social and the political, but on the contrary challenged unjust social realities, incorporating a very strong cosmological framework taken from the old tradition of the land (Amazonian life) and the new tradition (Christianity).

In an era in which most people declare themselves to be spiritual but not necessarily religious Casaldáliga's contribution to a future of Latin American theology is crucial. His ascent to the mountain of God, a well-known biblical metaphor related to the climbing required for reaching the Jerusalem Temple and the metaphor for contemplation used by the Spanish mystic St John of the Cross, outlines his whole life and theological contribution. Action and contemplation came together in his life, so that his pastoral work was active, meaningful and intense, rooted in a life of contemplation of God's creation and the tranquillity of the mystic who experiences God in the beauty of nature and longs for that emotion to become action, and not vice versa. Thus, Casaldáliga, a Spaniard, treasured the poems of St John of the Cross and the Carmelite tradition of ascent towards Mount Carmel in a contextual way, and thus wrote:

> If he [John of the Cross] had been a modern Latin American and had lived through the continental councils of Medellín, Puebla and Santo Domingo, John of the Cross might well – without betraying either holiness or poetry or orthodoxy – have written, as one possibility, the 'Ascent of Machu-Pichu': the ascent and the descent ...[59]

Within that personal spiritual journey towards God, Casaldáliga recognized that there were economic mistakes being made in Amazonia, particularly the increased cultivation of cotton and soy bean. It is because of his heightened spiritual journey into contemplation that he became conscious that the social conscience of the indigenous populations and of the Christian communities would make possible an ongoing challenge to the poor fruits of economic globalization. Ever an optimist, Casaldáliga encouraged people to take part in and to support what he called 'social movements' – what I would call civil society – thus encouraging the solidarity and action of Christians within wider organizations and within alliances that could embrace the majority of Christians of Brazil and civil organizations concerned with single issues of socio-political significance, such as land and ecological issues. It is for these reasons that Casaldáliga, without being in an academic setting, encouraged the ongoing development of a Latin American theology for the twenty-first century, a theology closely allied with social actions in the name of the values and attitudes required by God in order to bring people closer to the values and ethical attitudes represented in the Gospels through the Kingdom of God.

In one of his later pastoral letters, and one of the shortest pastoral letters, that of August 2006, he told of the pilgrimage to the martyrs of the *caminhada* at the shrine of Ribeirão Cascalheira on the occasion of the thirtieth anniversary of the martyrdom of Fr João Bosco Penido Burnier. By that time, a new bishop had been appointed to replace him, but he was still in Araguaia and he thanked many people who had written to him wishing him well and thanking him for years of companionship. Casaldáliga reminded them that the pilgrimage was not finished and that the central symbol of such *caminhada* continued to be the presence of martyrs within the region and within the communities.[60] It is that subversive martyrdom that remained the sign of the Kingdom within a Latin America that faced several presidential elections of some importance in Brazil, Chile and Ecuador.

For Casaldáliga, it is good that there is a vote but he wrote sharply, 'You can vote but you cannot be', meaning that even when finally Latin Americans could vote in the democratic polls their opinion didn't count as much as in the past because of all the economic policies implemented within contemporary globalization.[61] In his writings about the assassinated Archbishop of El Salvador, Oscar Romero, Casaldáliga considered him central to the life and to the spirituality of Latin Americans because of his prophetic vision and because of his life with and for the poor. However, he assessed the changes in Latin America as follows: 'from a national security state ordered and controlled by the military to the trans-national security capital, from the military dictatorships to the macro-dictatorship of the neo-liberal empire'.[62]

One of the characteristics shared by bishops such as Casaldáliga and Romero was the possibility of remaining part of the institutional Church and at the same time open to the Spirit, open to learning from the poor, open to the possible dangers of assuming that not everything in society was fine and that profit and the markets could not be at the centre of human life and human existence. The poverty of Romero and of Casaldáliga was the poverty of those who recognize that God is at the centre and the rest is secondary, the poverty of the Spirit to trust in hope that even if society seems to be collapsing altogether God is at the centre of the lives of all within a community-oriented pilgrimage towards God. For Casaldáliga the Church needs to confront the different kinds of terrorism, a phenomenon that didn't start with the attacks on New York and Washington DC on 9/11, but a phenomenon that appears everywhere when another human being is attacked by a single thief or by a system that confronts a human being with violence and terror. He proposed three concrete challenges for the Church that could connect the Church with the challenges of a contemporary world: (1) world decentralization, (2) responsible participation, and (3) dialogue in solidarity.[63] For the Church must bring hope to a world that has proclaimed 'the death of God', 'the end of humanity' and 'the end of history' by reminding all that God is still there and that there have been a wide variety of terrorisms throughout the ages.

For Casaldáliga hope lies within humanity, within human beings and their hopes, because God created this world and these human beings.[64] Hope does not lie within war machines or security strategies. His assessment of the first years of the new millennium communicate a sobering picture of events but a very hopeful human challenge embraced already by many. Thus, Casaldáliga wrote:

Two years of the new 21st century have already passed and the world continues to be cruel and in solidarity, unjust and hopeful. There is still war and there is still empire, and empire has invented preventative war. The world is still divided into at least three: First, Third, and Fourth. Hunger, poverty, corruption and violence have increased; but conscience, protest, organization, and the explicit will for alternatives have also increased.[65]

Within that mixed picture of insecurity and hope Casaldáliga continued speaking about another kind of terrorism, that spelled out by the United Nations Secretary General Kofi Annan, as systematic and tolerated, the terrorism of poverty created and sustained by the privileged nations unto all citizens of other less privileged nations.[66] Further, Casaldáliga's hope was expressed through his conviction that the twenty-first century would be a mystical and ecological century and that, as many empires collapsed, the American empire would collapse within this century.[67] If his statement could sound very subversive and problematic, it is because Casaldáliga embraced the absolute and non-negotiable centrality of the Kingdom of God and the immediate need to go left, to turn crisis into realities and to remain alive within Christianity, alive with challenges, with prayers, within a world that is in the making and needs to be shaped within God's love, solidarity and justice rather than within profit, markets and military security.[68] It is indeed a utopian world, a revolutionary world of mysticism and ideas that has enough members and enough authority to confront dreamers of worlds of poverty, injustice and inequality.

Despite those routinely addressed issues that could relate Christians of Brazil to other worlds' concerns, one of Casaldáliga's main priorities was always to encourage the participation of lay people within the Catholic Church and particularly the lay ministries of women within the Church. It is such a life of respect and dialogue with indigenous populations that Casaldáliga brought with him throughout his life. A bishop who cooked, washed his clothes by hand and welcomed with contagious hope all his visitors was hated by the landowners, who saw in him an obstacle to progress, in the words of the state, but an obstacle to their own enrichment in the words of Dom Pedro.

The death of Dom Pedro during the pandemic, in August 2020, was poignant to say the least because that was the year in which Francis had triggered reflections on the role of dialogue and the central role of indigenous populations in the contemporary world through his Apostolic Exhortation *Querida Amazonia*. Dom Pedro had been diagnosed with Parkinson's disease some years before, but he continued living in the same place as a priest, and enjoying the many guests who greeted him in Amazonia and who visited him from abroad.

Dialogue and respect for indigenous traditions and their forms of understanding the Divinity became coterminous for Dom Pedro. In his own history he brought together liberation theology and interreligious dialogue by expanding liberation and interreligious dialogue to a larger universe, that of Amazonia, rather than confining it to the religions of the book or Indian religions. He shared the living joy of spending most of his life in Amazonia, and Pope Francis described 'its splendour, its drama and its mystery'.[69] Within that mystery of Amazonian life, 'good living', *buen vivir*, with an ethical community lifestyle, provided an integral approach to 'good acting'.[70] But as Dom Pedro had indicated, for the past 30 years Amazonia has also been 'a place of suffering and violence'.[71] The following threats to life were outlined by the Amazonian pre-synod consultations:

appropriation and privatization of natural goods, such as water itself; legal logging concessions and illegal logging; predatory hunting and fishing; unsustainable mega-projects (hydroelectric and forest concessions, massive logging, mono cultivation, highways, waterways, railways, and mining and oil projects); pollution caused by extractive industries and city garbage dumps; and, above all, climate change. These are real threats with serious social consequences: pollution related diseases, drug trafficking, illegal armed groups, alcoholism, violence against women, sexual exploitation, human trafficking and smuggling, organ traffic, sex tourism, the loss of original culture and identity (language, customs and spiritual practices), criminalization and assassination of leaders and defenders of the territory.[72]

The death of Dom Pedro Casaldáliga the year after the Amazonian Synod, on 8 August 2020 (Batatais, State of São Paulo), brought life to the ongoing understanding of the poor and indigenous populations, who need liberation but who have also taught the Church about dialogue in a larger world of the Divinity in all its manifestations. The Provincial of the Claretians summarized such life, stating that Dom Pedro's life said it all. Because heaven and earth were not disassociated in his life, he shouted the dignity of the marginalized; few stressed prayer and the broken bread of the Eucharist as he did.[73]

In Chapters 3 and 4 I have outlined the basics of liberation theology so as to avoid any caricature of what its potential within contemporary contextual theologies is and the methodological tools used, that is, liberating praxis and orthopraxis. At the same time, I have argued that within the first generation of liberation theologians, and particularly within the life and work of Gutiérrez and Casaldáliga, an intense and creative interreligious dialogue took place. Therefore, social justice and action are usually connected to interreligious dialogue. However, the two areas of interreligious dialogue and liberation theology did not reflect on such connection because they were immersed in theologizing with the poor. Dialogue took place naturally between Christianity and Amazonian religions in the case of Casaldáliga, and such reflection opens new possibilities for the connections between liberation and dialogue. This has been a feature of religious communities during the pandemic, as outlined by Bishop Jorge Patricio Vega, Chilean bishop-in-charge of interreligious dialogue on behalf of the Chilean Episcopal Conference. On a fruitful dialogue between the Apostolic Nuncio to Chile, Bishop Vega of Illapel, Pastor Johannes Merkel of the Evangelical Lutheran Church of Chile, and Rabbi Shmuel Szteinhendler of the Beit Emunach community, Bishop Vega outlined the need for social justice within a very difficult moment for all citizens and clarified that the bishops had not been seen on television because they were working to help the poor and marginalized.[74] Such an event outlines some of the opportunities and some of the responsibilities in joining praxis and dialogue in a post-pandemic world.

Notes

1 Pontifical Council for the Family, 'Reflection by Card. Alfonso López Trujillo: On the anniversary of the Puebla Conference', 12 February 2004; cf. Paul VI, *Populorum Progressio*, 26 March 1967, Vatican City: Libreria Editrice Vaticana.

2 *Populorum Progressio*, § 23.

3 *Populorum Progressio*, § 23.

4 *Populorum Progressio*, § 23.

5 *Populorum Progressio*, § 23.

6 Neil L. Whitehead (ed.), *Histories and Historicities in Amazonia*, Lincoln: University of Nebraska Press, 2003.

7 Gutiérrez prefers the term 'encounter' or 'collision', while those reading history from a European view-point term it 'discovery' or 'conquest' and others even term it 'invasion' or 'covering'; Gustavo Gutiérrez, *Las Casas: In Search of the Poor of Jesus Christ*, Maryknoll, NY: Orbis, 1993, p. 2.

8 It was in that context that the Jesuits developed safe places around the borders of current Argentina, Paraguay and Brazil for indigenous peoples to live in well-bounded territories where they learned about Christianity, toiled the land, lived communally and escaped the enslaving mechanisms of the Portuguese slavers. The Jesuits were expelled from the Portuguese colonies in 1759, from France in 1762 and from the Spanish colonies in 1767. On 21 July 1773, Pope Clement XIV suspended the mere existence of the Society of Jesus; Michel Clévenot, 'The Kingdom of God on Earth? The Jesuit Reductions of Paraguay', *Concilium* 187 (1986), pp. 70–7; Leonardo Boff and Virgil Elizondo (eds), *Option for the Poor: Challenge to the Rich Countries*, Edinburgh: T&T Clark, 1986.

9 Gustavo Gutiérrez, *En busca de los pobres de Jesucristo*, Lima: Instituto Bartolomé de las Casas-Rimac and Centro de Estudios y Publicaciones, 1992.

10 However, Las Casas was not, according to Gutiérrez, an isolated prophetic voice but he was part of a minority group that included missionaries, bishops, civil servants and event members of the royal court

who expressed their concern about the fate of the Indians under the conquistadors; Gustavo Gutiérrez, *Las Casas*, p. 5.

11 Lewis Hanke, *Aristotle and the American Indians: A Study in Race Prejudice in the Modern World*, London: Hollis & Carter, Chicago: Henry Regnery, 1959, *All the Peoples of the World are Men: The Disputation between Bartolomé de Las Casas and Juan Ginés de Sepúlveda in 1550 on the Intellectual and Religious Capacity of the American Indians*, Minneapolis, MN: University of Minnesota Press, 1970; *All Mankind is One: A Study of the Disputation between Bartolomé de Las Casas and Juan Ginés de Sepúlveda in 1550 on the Intellectual and Religious Capacity of the American Indians*, Dekalb: Northern Illinois University Press, 1974.

12 Gustavo Gutiérrez, *On Job: God-Talk and the Suffering of the Innocent*, Maryknoll, NY: Orbis, 1987.

13 Gustavo Gutiérrez, *Las Casas*, pp. 6–7. Gutiérrez refers to Las Casas' account of the atrocities done by the conquistadors, *A Short Account of the Destruction of the Indies*, London: Penguin, with chronology and further reading, 2004 [1992].

14 Virgil Elizondo and Leonardo Boff, 'Editorial: Theology from the Viewpoint of the Poor', *Concilium* 187 (1986), p. ix; Boff and Elizondo (eds), *Option for the Poor*.

15 Virgilio Elizondo has argued, for example, that 'the transformative impact of the Medellín Conference on the church's pastoral practice and theology was far greater than that exercised by any other council of the church. No dogmas or confessions of faith were questioned or challenged – Protestant or Catholic. Instead, the whole edifice of Constantinian Christian thought, imagery, and symbolism was radically challenged in the name of Christianity itself. What was initiated was not a new academic or philosophical theology, but rather the transformation of the very structures and methods of doing theology. To be faithful and authentic, Christian theology will have to emerge out of the spiritual experience of the believing community grappling with its history and responding to its contemporary situation'; see 'Emergence of a World Church and the Irruption of the Poor', in Gregory Baum (ed.), *The Twentieth Century: A Theological Overview*, Maryknoll, NY: Orbis, 1999, p. 108.

16 See Mario I. Aguilar, *A Social History of the Catholic Church in Chile*, vol. I *The First Period of the Pinochet Government 1973–1980*, Lewiston, Queenston and Lampeter: Edwin Mellen Press, 2004.

17 Gustavo Gutiérrez, *Beber en su propio pozo: En el itinerario de un pueblo*, Lima: Centro de Estudios y Publicaciones, 1983; English translation, *We Drink from Our Own Wells: The Spiritual Journey of a People*, Maryknoll, NY: Orbis, 1984, 20th anniversary edn 2003.

18 Gustavo Gutiérrez, *The God of Life*, London: SCM Press, 1991, p. 2; Spanish original, *El Dios de la vida*, Lima: Centro de Estudios

y Publicaciones, 1982 (shorter version), Lima: Instituto Bartolomé de Las Casas-Rimac and Centro de Estudios y Publicaciones, 1989 (longer version).

19 Gutiérrez does not dwell on issues of contemplation, but those who did, for example Ernesto Cardenal and Pedro Casaldáliga, associated mysticism, aesthetics and poetics with a political commitment to social change inspired by their Christian commitment to the poor and the marginalized; see Ernesto Cardenal, *El Evangelio en Solentiname*, Salamanca: Ediciones Sígueme, 1976; and *El Evangelio en Solentiname: Volumen Segundo*, Salamanca: Ediciones Sígueme, 1978.

20 Paper presented at the first Hugo Echegaray University Seminar, organized by UNEC, in G. Gutiérrez, R. Ames, J. Iguiñez and C. Chipoco, *Sobre el trabajo humano: Comentarios a la Encíclica Laborem Exercens*, Lima: Centro de Estudios y Publicaciones, 1982.

21 Gustavo Gutiérrez, 'The Gospel of Work: Reflections on *Laborem Exercens*', in Gustavo Gutiérrez, *The Density of the Present: Selected Writings*, Maryknoll, NY: Orbis, 1999, p. 37.

22 Gregory the Great, Pastoral Rule, 3.21, in Gustavo Gutiérrez, 'New Things Today: A Rereading of *Rerum Novarum*', in Gutiérrez, *The Density of the Present*, p. 51, note 14. Most of these ideas were given by Gutiérrez at the Catholic University of Lima during the 'Jornadas de Teología' in February 1991.

23 Jon Sobrino SJ, 'El Cristianismo ante el siglo XXI en América Latina: Una reflexión desde las víctimas', in *Teología de la liberación: Cruce de miradas*, Coloquio de Friburgo, April 1999, Lima: Instituto Bartolomé de Las Casas-Rímac and Centro de Estudios y Publicaciones, 2000, pp. 207–38.

24 In 1999 Gutiérrez argued that 'Estamos ante una estimulante y prometedora tarea en la que la teología de la liberación tiene mucho que hacer, y sobre todo por aprender', in 'Situaciones y tareas de la teología de la liberación', *Teología de la liberación*, pp. 239–64, at p. 264.

25 Nicholas Lash, 'Theologies at the Service of a Common Tradition', *Concilium* 171 (1984), p. 74; Claude Geffré, Gustavo Gutiérrez and Virgil Elizondo (eds), *Different Theologies, Common Responsibility: Babel or Pentecost?*, Edinburgh: T&T Clark, 1984.

26 Gustavo Gutiérrez, 'Liberation Praxis and Christian Faith', in *The Power of the Poor in History: Selected Writings*, London: SCM Press, 1983, p. 36.

27 'The vanguard of Protestant theology would become the great Christian theology of modernity, for it was a current that would lend an attentive ear to the questions asked by critical reason and individual liberty in this society forged by the bourgeoisie. For a number of historical reasons, this theology would centre in Germany, the land of the Reformation'. Gutiérrez, 'Theology from the Underside of History', in *The Power of the Poor*, p. 178.

28 On Bonhoeffer, see Gustavo Gutiérrez, 'Theology from the Underside of History', pp. 179–81.

29 'It [the revolutionary struggle] insists in a society in which private ownership of the means of production is eliminated, because private ownership of the means of production allows a few to appropriate the fruits of the labour of many, and generates the division of society into classes, whereupon one class exploits another'. Gutiérrez, 'Liberation Praxis and Christian Faith', in The Power of the Poor, pp. 37–8.

30 Gutiérrez, 'Liberation Praxis and Christian Faith', in The Power of the Poor in History: Selected Writings, p. 65.

31 Frei Betto, 'Gustavo Gutiérrez – A Friendly Profile', in Marc H. Ellis and Otto Maduro (eds), The Future of Liberation Theology: Essays in Honor of Gustavo Gutiérrez, Maryknoll, NY: Orbis, 1989, pp. 31–7, at p. 36.

32 For a historical overview, see Luis Alberto Gómez de Souza, 'The Origins of Medellín: From Catholic Action to the Base Church Communities and Social Pastoral Strategy (1950–68)', in José Oscar Beozzo and Luiz Carlos Susin (eds), Brazil: People and Church(es), Concilium, 2002/3, pp. 31–7.

33 Peter Flynn, Brazil: A Political Analysis, London and Boulder, CO: Ernest Benn and Westview Press, 1978, pp. 308–65; and Alfred Stepan, Rethinking Military Politics: Brazil and the Southern Cone, Princeton, NJ: Princeton University Press, 1988.

34 Thomas E. Skidmore, 'Brazil's Slow Road to Democratization: 1974–1985', in Alfred Stepan (ed.), Democratizing Brazil: Problems of Transition and Consolidation, New York and Oxford: Oxford University Press, 1989, pp. 5–42.

35 Operación Cóndor comprised a network of intelligence services from the Southern Cone, most of them associated with the military regimes of the 1970s, that started after a meeting of delegates in Santiago in 1974. The general coordinator of the whole operation was General (retd) Manuel Contreras, head of the Chilean state intelligence services – DINA, known as Cóndor number 1; see Samuel Blixen, El vientre del cóndor: Del archivo del terror al caso Berríos, Montevideo: Brecha, 1994; Alfredo Boccia Paz, Miguel H. López, Antonio V. Pecci and Gloria Giménez Guanes, En los sótanos de los generales: Los documentos ocultos del Operativo Cóndor, Asunción: Expolibro/Servilibro, 2002; Stella Calloni, Los años del lobo: Operación Cóndor, Buenos Aires: Ediciones Continente, 1999; John Dinges, Operación Cóndor: Una década de terrorismo internacional en el Cono Sur, Santiago: Ediciones B, 2004; Nilson Cézar Mariano, Operación Cóndor: Terrorismo de estado en el Cono Sur, Buenos Aires: Lohlé-Lumen, 1998; and Francisco Martorell, Operación Cóndor: El vuelo de la muerte – La coordinación represiva en el Cono Sur, Santiago: LOM, 1999.

36 Scott Mainwaring, *The Catholic Church and Politics in Brazil 1916–1985*, Stanford: Stanford University Press, 1986.

37 Ralph Della Cava, 'The "People's Church", the Vatican and Abertura', in Stepan (ed.), *Democratizing Brazil*, pp. 143–67, at pp. 152–3.

38 W. E. Hewitt, *Base Christian Communities and Social Change in Brazil*, Lincoln and London: University of Nebraska Press, 1991; and Maria Helena Moreira Alves, *Estado e oposição no Brasil 1964–1984*, Petrópolis: Editora Vozes, 1984.

39 Thomas C. Bruneau, *The Political Transformation of the Brazilian Catholic Church*, New York: Cambridge University Press, 1974; and *The Church in Brazil*, Austin, TX: University of Texas Press, 1982; Cardinal Aloísio Lorscheider, 'Fifty Years of the CNBB: A Bishop's Conference Based on the Council – Evangelization Projects, Political and Ecclesiastical Tensions and Challenges', in Beozzo and Susin (eds), pp. 25–30.

40 Pedro Casaldáliga, '2000 Years of Jesús, 20 Years of Romero: A Fraternal Circular Letter', São Félix do Araguaia, 2000.

41 The Claretian missionaries were founded in Vic, Spain, on 16 July 1849 by a group of young priests led by Antonio Claret, later to become Archbishop of Cuba, 20 days after the foundation of this new missionary congregation. The official name of the Claretian missionaries is the Congregation of Missionary Sons of the Immaculate Heart of Mary. Anthony Mary Claret was canonized by the Vatican on 7 May 1950, and today Claretian missionaries have 2,000 members working in 61 countries.

42 Pedro Casaldáliga, *Yo creo en la justicia y en la esperanza: El credo que ha dado sentido a mi vida*, Bilbao: Desclée de Brouwer, 1976; English translation published as *I Believe in Justice and Hope*, Notre Dame, IN: FIDES-Claretian, 1978.

43 Teófilo Cabestrero, *Diálogos en Mato Grosso con Pedro Casaldáliga*, Salamanca: Sígueme, 1978, English translation published as *Mystic of Liberation: A Portrait of Bishop Pedro Casaldáliga of Brazil*, Maryknoll, NY: Orbis, 1981.

44 Pedro Casaldáliga, 'Open Letter to the Soul of Brazil', in Beozzo and Susin (eds), *Brazil*, pp. 123–8 at p. 123.

45 Pedro Casaldáliga, 'Una Igleja de Amazonia em conflito com o latifundio e marginalização social', 23 October 1971; see also Pedro Casaldáliga, *Tierra nuestra, libertad*, Buenos Aires: Editorial Guadalupe, 1974.

46 For the twenty-fifth anniversary of the priest's assassination, Casaldáliga organized a one-day pilgrimage that started with a shared lunch on 14 July and ended with a shared lunch the following day, 15 July 2001; see Pedro Casaldáliga, 'Vidas por la causa: Romería de los mártires de la caminada', 14–15 July 2001, Ribeirão Cascalheira, Prelatura de São Féliz do Araguaia, MT, Brazil.

47 Vasconcelos Quadros, 'El Obispo de los excluídos', *Familia Cristiana*, October 2002.

48 Domingo Oriol, 'Entrevista a Pedro Casaldáliga', *La Vanguardia* (Barcelona), Thursday 13 January 2005.

49 Pedro Casaldáliga, 'But the Wind Continues', circular letter, February 2005, São Félix do Araguaia.

50 On that occasion the Portuguese translation of his biography, originally written in Catalan, was launched and Casaldáliga asserted that he liked to remain on the red soil, the distinctive colour of the Amazonian soil; see Francesc Escribano, *Descalç sobre la terra vermella: Vida del bisbe Pere Casaldáliga*, Barcelona: Edicions 62, 1999; Portuguese translation published as *Descalço sobre a terra vermelha*, São Paulo, 2000; Spanish translation published as *Descalzo sobre la tierra roja: Vida del Obispo Pedro Casaldáliga*, Barcelona: Ediciones Península, 2000.

51 Casaldáliga played with the term *honoris causa* and insisted that his doctorate was *passionis causa* because of his passion for utopia.

52 The theme of the Kingdom of God connects all of his works; see Pedro Casaldáliga, *Al acecho del Reino: Antología de textos 1968–1988*, Madrid: Nueva Utopía and Ediciones Endymión, 1989, and Mexico City: Claves Latinoamericanas, 1990; English translation, *In Pursuit of the Kingdom: Writings 1968–1988*, Maryknoll, NY: Orbis, 1990.

53 Pedro Casaldáliga, 'I Believe in Resurrection', in Andrés Torres Queiruja, Luiz Carlos Susin and Jon Sobrino (eds), *The Resurrection of the Dead*, Concilium 2006/5, London: SCM Press, pp. 121–3, at p. 123.

54 Pedro Casaldáliga, 'Declaración de amor a la revolución total de Cuba'.

55 Pedro Casaldáliga and José María Vigil, *Espiritualidad de la liberación*, São Paulo: CESEP – São Paulo and Ediciones Paulinas, 1993; English translation published as *The Spirituality of Liberation*, Liberation and Theology 12, Tunbridge Wells: Burns & Oates, and Maryknoll, NY: Orbis, 1994.

56 Gutiérrez, *Beber en su propio pozo*, English translation, *We Drink From Our Own Wells*. Other Latin Americans working on a more traditional vein of spirituality include Segundo Galilea and his works *Aspectos críticos en la espiritualidad actual*, Bogotá: Indo-American Press Service, 1975; *El camino de la espiritualidad*, Bogotá: Ediciones Paulinas, 1983, *El futuro de nuestro pasado: Ensayo sobre los místicos españoles desde América Latina*, Bogotá: CLAR, 1983; and *Espiritualidad de la liberación*, Santiago: ISPAJ, 1973, and Bogotá: CLAR, 1979.

57 Mario I. Aguilar, *The History and Politics of Latin American Theology*, vol. I, ch. 5: 'Ernesto Cardenal', London: SCM Press, 2007.

58 Pedro Casaldáliga, *En rebelde fidelidad, Diario 1977–1983*, Bilbao: Desclée de Brouwer, 1983.

59 Casaldáliga and Vigil, *The Spirituality of Liberation*, pp. xv–xvi.

60 Pedro Casaldáliga, *Orações da caminhada*, Campinas, SP: Editora Verus, 2005.

61 Pedro Casaldáliga, 'La romería continúa', São Félix do Araguaia, MT, Brazil, August 2006.

62 Pedro Casaldáliga, 'Carta abierta al hermano Romero', 24 March 2005.

63 Pedro Casaldáliga, 'El mundo vuelve a empezar', *Circular Fraterna*, 2002.

64 Pedro Casaldáliga, *Cartas marcadas*, São Paulo: Paulus, 2005.

65 Pedro Casaldáliga, 'In the Dark Hour of the Dawn', *Circular Fraterna*, 2003.

66 Pedro Casaldáliga, 'Pasar haciendo caminos', *Circular Fraterna*, April 2004.

67 Pedro Casaldáliga, 'Utopía necesaria como el pan de cada día', *Circular Fraterna*, January 2006.

68 Pedro Casaldáliga, *Cuando los días dan que pensar: Memoria: ideario, compromiso*, Madrid: PPC, 2005.

69 *Querida Amazonia*, § 1.

70 Synod of Bishops, Special Assembly for the Pan-Amazonian Region, 'The Amazon: New Paths for the Church and for an Integral Ecology – Final Document', Vatican, 26 October 2019, § 9.

71 Synod of Bishops, Special Assembly for the Pan-Amazonian Region, 'Final Document', § 10.

72 Synod of Bishops, Special Assembly for the Pan-Amazonian Region, 'Final Document', § 10.

73 www.vaticannews.va/es/iglesia/news/2020-08/pedro-casaldaliga-su-vida-habla-sola-carta-superior-claretiano.html, accessed 31.8.20.

74 'Las religiones ante los desafíos del mundo post pandemia', a conversation online organized by different faith communities in Chile, 20 August 2020, with the participation of faith communities from different Latin American countries.

5

A Post-Pandemic Theology of
Multiple Belonging

If liberation theology and interreligious dialogue have come together during the pandemic it is because they theologically reflect God's unity. To love the poor and to act for them comes together with the marginalized who in many cases are marginalized because of their religious practice and faith. Pope Francis has clearly advanced faith communities working together and has pushed the action of the Church as the sacrament of God to the peripheries, borders and locations where marginalization takes place. Within such a post-pandemic agenda and within this chapter I argue for a diversification of socio-theological issues to be looked at within a multiple belonging to a shared humanity in universal responsibility.

Pandemic Movements towards Enclaves and Borders

In her ongoing work, Arpita Chakraborty has explored the realities of those who by political partitions, appropriation and border-creations have become stateless and without nationality: people of the *enclaves* who came out of the Partition of India and the creation of Pakistan and of Bangladesh, the enclaves of Bengal.[1] As the political partitions of Bengal took place over time and Pakistan and Bangladesh were created on a map, people of the enclaves became part of one country but hosted in another without rights in the location where they were and no identity that could prove any entitlement.[2] This could be just a sociological fact in the Durkheimian sense, and as such it would be important. However, Chakraborty has provided their voice and has called for further research not only on borderlands but also on bordered identities. For the identity of those of enclaves is that of settlers hosted by one country but with roots in another, with no identity card and therefore no rights and no state facilities in another country. Thus, the strategy pursued by women, for example, in a Bangladeshi enclave was to be part of an arranged marriage with an Indian citizen, thus offering full Indian nationality rights on the legal act of marriage. In this case, praxis becomes a moment of empathy in which, in a wider world divided by nationality rights, the poor and the marginalized are not only those who are discriminated against through social differentiation but those who do not have legal existence because of state expansions and political movements. The realities of such social existence should be plentiful but subjects at the borders and at the margins only appear within the literature when they are part of a larger discussion, a problem for the state, or a social category to be aided in order to become something else, somebody else, mainly through the wishes of others.

Theologically, such subjects do not appear within European contextual theology (systematic theology) because they are social facts and God within systematic theology does not seem to operate within social facts but in sacred and textualized realities. There is plentiful evidence in the Gospels that Jesus of Nazareth busied himself with such realities and that the first Christians in Jerusalem and Rome were part of those enclaves. They didn't have Roman nationality (with the exception of Paul and some Roman soldiers who converted to the Way) and they developed a sense of the 'coming of God' and the 'reign of God', despite the many changes and the many partitions that took place around them.[3] They were concerned with widows and orphans and with their prayers, the sharing of bread and the sense of serving God, rather than with the building of further temples so as to compete with the Roman state religion and the many gods around them.

Such social perspective and theological reflection about God go beyond the liberation expected by the first generation of liberation theologians in Latin America, whereby the perception, conception and awareness of a world was limited and limiting. In fact, essence, origin and reception as theological phenomena need to be separated in any given argument and theological analysis. Latin American theologians were concerned about political injustice, progress and developments, all during the first generation dictated by men and clerics who were at the forefront of a world that didn't include in its reflections those at the margins. The poor were at the centre of Gutiérrez' theology but didn't appear within the combined reflections of a liberation theology that was spearheaded by publishers in the English language and became a bestseller and a subject that caused either enthusiastic support or utter rejection. Thus, even the perception of states and borders has ended, because the state as an orderly and limiting border has already ended theologically and sociologically. Nationalism and nationality are non-vectors of meaning but contained structures where the citizen operates. The multiplicity of belonging, I would argue, arises not out of the nation-structures or out of the symbolic structures of belonging to one community but out of an awareness and living of a larger humanity. As I have already outlined previously, the Kingdom of God in Christianity provides the opening to a world in which God certainly is larger than our borders and limits because, otherwise, she would be limited and would not be God. Thus, our fresh contemporary reflection is not only on the method of liberation theology (praxis), but on its 'truth' (orthopraxis) and its location (belonging).[4]

And it is in that location, in diversity and multiple belonging, that I embrace the full spectrum of liberation theologies, from the traditional Latin American liberation theology to post-structuralist feminism, to the latest and all-embracing interreligious agenda outside Christian theologies, proposed by the contributors to *Post-Christian Interreligious Liberation Theology*, 'that are not replicate at all of Christian or Latin American liberation theology'.[5] Indeed, I agree with the contributors to that volume that liberation theology could be used as a methodology and a critical way of thinking within other traditions outside Christianity. Indeed, one of the criticisms towards

Miguel De La Torre's contribution to liberation theology could be that in the context of the USA it outlined the plausibility of a way of doing theology in which the over-emphasis is on the 'truth' of Christianity.[6] This is not surprising with the rising of the Christian Right and with an ongoing US tension between a secular constitutional country and the Christian lobby, the ignorance and misunderstanding of Islam and the exclusion of other world religions as part of the nation.[7] I share such mild criticism with the editors of the volume *Post-Christian Interreligious Liberation Theology*, particularly when it comes to the portrayal of Islam and Muslims after 9/11. I outlined such concerns in the context of the history of Latin American theology and the allied attack and invasion of Iraq in 2003, at a time when Elsa Támez led a campaign not to visit the USA for conferences or invited lectures.[8] In her reply to Támez, Rosemary Ruether outlined her support for such protests from US feminist theologians, stating:

> I believe that travel boycotts by theologians, church leaders and academics can be one important gesture in that direction. Like the academic boycott of travel to South Africa during the apartheid years, such gestures need to operate in concert with many other strategies of boycott and alternative organizing.[9]

The use of force once again in the Middle East, and the rising of the Christian Right and a somehow conservative representation of the message of the gospel, had also been used to invoke a God who is not the God of one nation but of all humanity.[10] However, in the case of the world religions, Miguel De La Torre and I shared a mild comparative attempt at introducing concepts common but very different within the world religions, with an emphasis on religions of the text by him and my very tentative comparison between 'liberation' in Christianity and Buddhism.[11] However, these are shades of a theological grey in that we belong to different Christian traditions and therefore the shade of 'truth' is expressed in very diverse ways.

Post-pandemic Theological Praxis

It is worth mentioning here that there are three moments in time and space that have prepared the ground for this post-pandemic action of learning once again from the poor and the marginalized, that connect very well with the solidarity of a suffering humanity post-pandemic and the very welcome theological explorations on world religions by their own practitioners, coordinated at the American Academy of Religion by Timani and Ashton with the encouragement of Francis X. Clooney, a shared central player in all these initiatives. The ongoing world crisis triggered by the pandemic will affect churches' structures and the availability of funds, donors and recipients of knowledge. The lack of open spaces where people can gather to celebrate their faith will have an impact on the usual ways of being church through buildings and Sunday gatherings. This will affect particularly faith communities where the Eucharist is kept within a building as a divine presence through the Blessed Sacrament. There is hope that in such a post-pandemic world the lessons learned from the pandemic through suffering and instability will bring us together, hopefully within a human multiple belonging, in a cosmic dance of many elements, including nature and the cosmos, animals, plants and different kinds of sexualities. May the day come when a Muslim and a Christian dance together for peace and understanding, praising the One God.

Within such multiplicity of the Divine and the human I would argue that theological praxis and theological reflection still look like a tense communion of senseless divisions. For the fact is that my experience was the same as that of many in Latin America, Africa and Asia: praxis is carried out by women, while committees and great published theologians are for the most part men. Thus, the project of publication of volumes on liberation theology years ago didn't come to an immediate fruition simply because, with others, I realized that in trying to ground the project within important milestones in theology, hosted by De Gruyter, the same people were invited. Most of them were male clerics whose books and thoughts were already available at the stalls of the annual meeting of the American Academy of Religion. Thus, we need to challenge in a post-pandemic climate our own praxis of theology by showing how ignorant we are in our theological curricula. Theology needs liberation because it has become a repetition of arguments that within a liberating praxis and interreligious dialogue have resembled many times a volume of historical theology rather than a contextual, pastoral, practical and political theology.

Women and their praxis and orthodoxy have a place within the reflection of the North, even when their role in ecclesiological praxis is less prominent, as I have been reminded many times by pioneers in these areas, but mostly from the North. Women theologians through the pandemic have been reminded of how traditional households are, as women have had the majority of the household chores and home schooling, to the detriment of their research and writing time. Women theologians from other continents do not appear in theological reading lists and are not discussed in theological conferences. I understand that the transition towards a theologically accepted South could probably bring a chaotic situation of change within the major Western Christian traditions, but it needs to happen. The work by Eve Parker, Anderson Jeremiah, Peniel Rajkumar and Rajbharat Patta, among other authors that have influenced my thinking, have pointed to socio-cultural and educational changes that need to happen if liberation theology and interreligious dialogue are to become part of the praxis and orthopraxis of churches and theologians in Africa, Asia and the UK.[12]

I recognize that I have been influenced by their work, their faith commitment and their challenge to a theological world that seems to be less liberating than years ago and might become irrelevant and extinct after the pandemic. We have debated the praxis of engagement between Christianity and Hinduism with intensity, and the sense that 'multiple belonging' can and cannot be part of the post-Panikkar world of interfaith dialogue. Dialogue or compromise? State-belonging or Kingdom without structures? Local theologies or global movements? These are areas that we debated with intensity over piles of food and even angry exchanges before the pandemic. How do we act inclusively after the pandemic? This is not material, I am afraid, for another conference with a document to follow, but this is life, and the difficult and complex life of liberation theologians involved in interreligious dialogue. The work by Dalit theologians brings together the tensions between liberation and dialogue, in that those involved in praxis are the churches and their members in Tamil Nadu but the theologians, predominantly males, are outside the social structures that from liberation theology could be considered agents of 'structural sin'.

My after-pestilence theological reflections are not a compendium of historical developments but a challenge to liberation theologians and to those involved in interfaith dialogue to come together because the Kingdom of God brings acceptance of diversity and social justice at the same time. I cannot provide a quick answer to these developments as everything has become less certain during the pandemic, but the possibilities that are present within a post-pandemic world are enormous, challenging and apocalyptic. After losing control of structures and the near future, all institutional theologians are forced to address the reports on 'praxis' as quickly as possible, as they have become changeable and non-orthodox in times of insecurity and solidarity. Cooperation with the poor and learning from the poor and marginalized has become by force the way of doing theology today. Once again, I am reminded of the first Christians who in their conversations with Paul the apostle expected the return of the Lord soon; as centuries passed Christians became less certain of an immediate return of the Lord and of their own transient journey on earth. It could be argued that our sense of the centrality of the Lord has been tampered with by our need to succeed. For the Black Book is not central to our lives if it creates a selfish sense of my personal salvation and as an effect disassociates liberation from love, and orthodoxy from human and divine diversity.

Women, Liberation, the Majority Churches

Where are the women? They were the ones who brought the news of the Lord's body as missing and told the apostles about its disappearance. They are the ones who have been, as mothers and homemakers, involved in the praxis of the Kingdom. They have protested the lack of food, rights and acceptance, then and now. And while social structures have played against their presence, they are the theologians of today in every community and in every church because they teach generations of children from when they are babies and bring life and purity from within their wombs. In terms of partitions and sexual violence, I have outlined the importance of the womb and purity vis-à-vis wells and locations, in order to add some socio-cultural meaning and historical explanation at moments of violence such as the 1947 Partition of India.

In a post-pandemic world, a liberating praxis of interreligious dialogue requires the voices of women and of others, including transgender people. They have been present in the actions for liberating women and education, at least within Africa and Latin America, and they are I am sure present in Asia while less prominent in the contemporary public sphere. Thus, I am not arguing for a new agenda for women – after all, I am a heterosexual man – but I am returning to the inclusiveness of a divine being and the Kingdom of God, which in our social battles we have sometimes forgotten. Theologies of the body and feminist theology have become historical theologies, given society's new understandings of LGBT people and of the exclusion of black men and women. I include all women in a liberating praxis because I include all traditions, all countries and societies within that Kingdom of God. However, I would like to point out some of those women who, in the South, have been public voices of such liberating praxis and who are less accepted in the theological curricula of today's limited ortho-dox world. Indeed, women theologians are working within the area of liberation theology because they themselves have had to organize their voices in order to be heard. This brings me to areas that I hope would never become canonical within theology but that are challenging when it comes to clear classifications and divisions between liberation theology, feminist theology, and postcolonial theology.

Great women theologians from the Global South have managed to incorporate liberation, feminist and postcolonial theologies, but in the case of Africa and Asia post-colonial theologies could be considered liberation theologies. This assumption comes from a socio-cultural climate of liberating praxis in which the colonial powers (over)stayed in Asia and Africa until the twentieth century, while the kingdom of Spain left Latin America in the first part of the nineteenth century. Three theologians emerge out of this all-inclusive and all-encompassing diverse world of multiple belonging: Marcella Althaus-Reid, Kwok Pui-lan, and Mercy Amba Oduyoye, the latter known as 'the mother of African women's theology'.[13] It is clear that women were not allowed to criticize the social order that culturally became over centuries the structural order of Christian traditions and churches. Hence the pioneering effort by Mercy Amba Oduyoye, who founded the Circle of Concerned African Women Theologians in 1988.[14] That experience of women, experience that I cannot have as a man, has been crucial in the community-oriented, radical challenge to patriarchy, to postcolonialism and to the ways of education, reading the Scriptures and the hierarchical running of Christian churches and diverse traditions within Christianity in the southern hemisphere.

If African women theologians seemed to have been forgotten, Asian women's voices seemed not to be prominent or challenging the given primacy of the seminal work on liberating Asia by Aloysius Pieris SJ on theological bookshelves.[15] With a first publication in German, Pieris argued in the manner of the first Latin American theologians for an identification with the poor, and with an Asian centrality on spirituality brought to theological fruition by the praxis of becoming poor with the poor.[16] Thus, his question dominated the Christian response to poverty, injustice and under-development: 'To be poor as Jesus was poor?' – with 'spirituality as a struggle for the poor'.[17] Further, in his own context of Asia he explored the liberating side of the non-Christian religions in the development of third world theology.[18] Well-known classical developments regarding other kinds of salvation theology were present in the works by Tissa Balasuriya and Raimon Panikkar. They followed liberating explorations on the role and presence of the Christ on an Asian continent in which the majority follow religions other than Christianity, except for the Philippines.

Was it the persecution by Josef Ratzinger of Balasuriya that triggered a certain absence of works on liberation theology in Asia?[19] Balasuriya was the founder of the Ecumenical Association of Third World Theologians and he published, in 1990, his work *Mary and Human Liberation*. In 1994 the Sri Lankan bishops warned that the book included heretical absences on the doctrine of original sin and on the divinity of Christ.[20] Balasuriya submitted a defence of his work to the Sacred Congregation for the Doctrine of the Faith, which was rejected. In May 1986 he was asked to adhere to a profession of faith prepared for him, which included the will to 'adhere with religious submission of will and intellect to the teachings of the Roman Pontiff'. Balasuriya submitted a profession of faith written by Paul VI, which was rejected, and he was excommunicated on 2 January 1997. After international publicity and pressure, his excommunication was lifted in January 1998. His later work on theologies of the cosmos was published among the lifting of other theological investigations that included Gustavo Gutiérrez and Leonardo Boff. However, his book on the Eucharist confirmed that a male liberation theologian was critically challenging how the Eucharist could be used to support colonization, sexism and racism.[21]

Asian Women Theologians

The voices of the third world and the voices of those who have relocated from Asia to other continents pose a problem for geographically located contextual theologies. Thus, one way of separating liberation theologies by those who have lived outside their formative contexts is to argue that liberation theologies are not always contextual theologies, while systematic theology could very possibly be known solely as a European contextual theology. These are not semantic discussions but they are at the centre of the encounter between liberation theologies and theologies of interreligious dialogue. The context of Christianity as a minority religion in Asia, for example, within a country in which most of the world religions are present, allows for a hybrid dialogue between the praxis of liberation and the orthopraxis of dialogue. This is because praxis assumes social injustice and symbolic systems that discriminate, such as caste, while dialogue becomes a sign of liberation because in praxis such dialogue does not exist. In praxis, solidarity with the poor and the oppressed is predicated upon a principle of social injustice and structural sin because the social structures are predicated upon a social injustice that arises out of the socio-political understanding of a text, that is, the Code of Manu, used by Hindus in order to exclude some from the equality granted to all by the constitution of India. Manu cannot be rejected by a minority because it is used by a majority, but it can be corrected in its interpretation under state developments and universal laws of equality. The equality of women culturally misunderstood as non-equality can only be challenged by a reaffirmation of all humans as equal and their dignity central to the human project of the state and the churches.

The praxis of Asian women theologians has not been a philosophical project of unity and diversity but an act of liberating women within a real experience of social injustice and the possibilities of changing such inequality from a dialogue about the past, in the present and for the future. What follows is my own choice of Asian women theologians and their contribution to such liberating dialogue over the years – somebody else would have other choices. My dividing principle of authority is of locality in Asia rather than the pre-eminence of publishing ventures in Europe or North America because of the primacy of praxis over reflection and our understanding of theology as a narrative about God that comes out of a second step, the first step being praxis.

The connection with the World Council of Churches and other church-related institutions is clear in this development of praxis and dialogue. For example, Aruna Gnanadason was coordinator of the Women's Program of the World Council of Churches, a member of the Church of South India, who in her writings linked the praxis of women in ecology and the ecumenical dialogue that comes from local cultures, globalization and faith. In *Listen to the Women! Listen to the Earth!* she outlined the conditions in which women play a significant role in the stewardship of creation by seeking a meeting between liberation theology, social justice and eco-feminist theologies.[22] She outlines the ongoing challenge faced by 'eco-systems people' in trying to preserve nature within a corporate understanding and economic doctrines that argue that nature is an object to be exploited. Thus, the praxis of a local liberation and the integrity of God's creation create a dialogue whereby the image of God comes out of the dialogue with indigenous peoples and particularly women. Further, in her eco-feminist ethic of resistance she argues for an ethic of care and prudence, while resisting development, with God's creation in mind.[23] Thus, her liberating praxis argues for Christians and churches as agents of transformation. In her work on women in the World Council of Churches she outlines the praxis of the difficulties that women go through with the support of the WCC; however, it is the stubbornness of Mary Magdalene on Easter morning at the tomb that theologically comes out of such praxis, so that 'Mary refused to leave the grave, even after the disciples had scattered in fear. She was not ready to accept that Jesus was no longer with them.'[24] Exclusion and violence takes place, but women continue their actions for social justice and the care of the planet. Gnanadason, together with Musimbi Kanyoro and Lucia McSpadden, has fostered reflections on women as agents of conflict resolution, with case studies from the Cameroon, Dominican Republic and India.[25]

The biblical challenges to a liberating praxis have also been central to theologies of liberation and postcolonial theologies since the ground-breaking work of Sugirtharajah.[26] The idea of a different hermeneutic and interpretive world in Asia made sense in his work, but it was certainly challenged by academic colleagues with no sense that the same challenge of colonial paradigms was possible within the guiding lights of the Black Book. Thus, biblical hermeneutics became an area where praxis, and an Asian liberating praxis, was to fulfil the plausibility of the Kingdom of God. Havilah Dharamraj, Old Testament scholar in Bangalore, has focused on the praxis of education and ministry training.[27] Dharamraj in India and Eve Parker in England develop the same criticism towards the limitations of a standard European education for ministers working with minorities or the Global South. The limitations of Western theological education are obvious when it comes to the majority churches, and Dharamraj has been central to this challenging moment that would not have been part of a colonial world. Questions about the PhD degree for theological education make me unsettled, having spent all my life forming students through PhDs, but this critique is extremely important and prophetic. 'Is there a PhD involved in three years of praxis on the fields of dreams of southern India?', I asked myself as I read the challenging critique by Dharamraj, who has questioned whether the shift from the Global North to the Global South has really been noticed by most European divinity schools. I can see that we are only two members of staff among 40 in St Andrews who engage with great joy in learning from scholars of the Global South, for example from Indian theologians and Christian communities. Dharamraj's contribution has been wider in Old Testament, particularly on the Song of Songs, with all the possibilities of intimacy and remorse in inter-human and divine–human relationships.[28] Dharamraj's intertextual analysis focuses not only on the production but on the reception of texts, setting the text alongside other portrayals of intimacy and liberation such as Hosea, Ezekiel and Isaiah. Indeed, her larger engagement with a South Asian Bible Commentary outlined a larger project of contextual and liberating engagement with the biblical text at the point of reception.[29] Indeed, her work of biblical reception is also complemented with her hermeneutics of formation and historical narrative in her detailed exegesis of Elijah in an intercessory role as important as that of Moses.[30] Thus, Dharamraj's work provides a liberation from textual monothematic analyses that contextually find it difficult to depart from the compilation of tradition within contexts that are located outside the European formal analysis. Dialogically, her work provides seminal foundations for textual dialogue in an Asiatic context.

In following literary praxis and liberation, and my reading of Nadia Murad (see Chapter 2), the contribution of the Indonesian Henriette Marianne Katoppo remains a central point of encounter for praxis, feminism and the novel, a forgotten point of empathic representation and intertextuality that I have tried to rescue within my work.[31] Katoppo outlines God's representation of God as mother and Mary as the complete woman. In the 1970s, and when any of these subjects were not part of the Asian daily vocabulary, Katoppo made a significant impact in Indonesia with her novels, and her work *Raumanenwon* won first prize at the Jakarta Arts Council Novel Competition. Within her novel, explorations of religion and ethnicity become part of the journey of a couple who are deeply in love, so that Monang, a Batak man, falls in love with a softer Minahasa woman who in her softness outlines the power of being a woman in setting forbidden boundaries and the agency of the feminine.[32] For it is in literature, a topic almost unknown in liberation theology, that empathy and personal connectiveness can actually arise and take place, as I have outlined in the case of genocide and in my forthcoming work on liberation theology and biography/autobiography and biographies of suffering.[33] In the creative self of the non-identified but of the ever-searching selfhood without attached roles, Katoppo as a new Frida Kahlo within theology explores the possibilities of a free Christian woman in Asia.[34] How free can such a being be? For her, such freedom is not a new invention but a right, and particularly the right to reject identities borrowed from men and from other cultural socio-symbolic creations. Her theological thinking reminded me of a first-year student who spoke to me after my lecture on caste within Hinduism and told me that her mother and she were not bound by such categories. After a long conversation, both of us realized that having been raised as a young woman of the elite she had been sheltered from social categories created by others. Katoppo, in her theological creativity, asks questions about those categories, remaining suspicious of men's plans for her, as well as stereotypes from other lands that seemed to signify God the Mother's freedom but in the end didn't. Thus, her work *Compassionate and Free*, when originally published by Orbis, was one of the first to use Asian myths and stories in theology supporting the image of God as Mother.[35]

There is no doubt that political and violent events in Asia have influenced the questions posed by Asian women theologians. Events on the barricades in the Philippines, violence in Myanmar, civil strife in Sri Lanka and ethnic violence throughout Asia have allowed women theologians to rethink categories of patriarchy, noise and silence within conflicts that otherwise, and from a male theological perspective, were the realm of state policies, revolutions and ideological change. A poignant hermeneutical question and challenge to European interpretation was already outlined by Sugirtharajah when he questioned the plausibility of the 'quest for the historical Jesus' as done in Europe as the only possibility. Thus, in a very diverse, historical and erudite volume, *Jesus in Asia*, Sugirtharajah gave us the wisdom of history and narrative within reception and context in a very complex hermeneutical milieu. I can hear some colleagues in Europe stating the obvious: how do you dare ask such questions? Or further, the reception of the texts cannot contradict the formation or the canonical history of the texts. Anna Sui Hluan, from Myanmar, for example, asked such difficult questions in her doctoral work on the issue of silence in 1 Corinthians 14.34–35 in the context of the traditional understanding of silence in Burmese society.[36] The Pauline texts assume silence for women in the community, and in the context of Burmese society such silence applies culturally to all women vis-à-vis individuals in authority. Such silencing of women was emphasized by missionaries, particularly by Adoniram Judson, who was the most influential because of his work in Bible translation.[37] Hluan asked what would be the appropriate contextualized practice for this Pauline passage, in her own contextual fear that after completing her studies she would not be allowed to be a leader within the Church.[38] Hluan not only challenged the translation from the Greek by Adorinam but also explored the possibilities of feminist and contextual hermeneutics appropriate for the context of Myanmar. She notes that, because of the restricted interaction between Myanmar and the West since the time of independence, there are no contextual theologies from the standpoint of Myanmar.[39] Apart from silence as cultural parameter of understanding, in which women were expected to be wives, mothers and daughters, the practice of polygamy was also part of traditional society in Myanmar. Hluan, after assessing the missionary translations and several hermeneutical methods to assess text formation and text reception, concludes that 'Paul's comment on women's silence in 1 Corinthians 14:34–36 is situationally specific and thus normative only for the specific situation in Corinth at that time'.[40]

The battles of biblical hermeneutics faced in Myanmar by an Evangelical theologian are no different from those faced by women theologians in physical barricades outside churches. In the Philippines, a country predominantly Catholic, the theological concerns have been less connected with the rest of Asia and interfaith dialogue, but issues of the person of Jesus for Asia and Christology have been at the centre of such theological concerns. After the pandemic, some of those concerns regarding human and sex trafficking, ethics and social justice, poverty and the development of women's rights, dignity and education, will remain at the centre of such a post-pandemic world. Will we have the courage to address them? And among the poor and the marginalized? One of those theologians at the barricades in the Philippines was Melba Padilla Maggay, who was instrumental in organizing the Protestant presence at the EDSA barricades during the People Power Uprising in February 1986. The ongoing challenge to Ferdinand Marcos ended with his removal and a campaign of civil resistance that led to the installation of Corazon Aquino as President of the Philippines.[41] Melba Maggay combined social sciences and theology in order to reflect on people's power, the possibilities of a gospel-led protest organizing the barricades, and the evangelical Protestant presence at such confrontation with the Marcos regime.[42] While she agrees with the possible limitations of a people's power, she argues strongly that emancipation and change only take place within the roots of a society whose core is religious.[43] Indeed, the example of the Philippines has not been allied to other societies in Asia where Christianity is a minority religion, while evangelical Christianity is not the majority religion in the Philippines.[44]

Liberating Praxis and the Orthodoxy of Dialogue

It could be argued that liberation theologians and theologians of interfaith dialogue have met at the barricades, at the points where the Kingdom is proclaimed through narratives of social justice. However, in most contexts those works for liberation in praxis have been allies with the ecumenical movement and with those wanting to understand the presence of the Divinity within a diversified variety of religions, be they large international bodies or a contextual indigenous movement. I would argue very strongly that a liberating praxis of the past was also a sectarian Christian movement, while in the contemporary globalized world liberation theologies need to rescue the Beatitudes and the globalized context, a context that is subdued within the social context present in the colonial Roman Empire at the time of the first Christians. They shared everything, witnessed to the resurrection of the Lord and advanced the values of the Kingdom within a large world, a diverse and varied world, with the apostles ending up in other lands, including Rome, under Roman persecution.[45] Within such ancient and contemporary worlds, small communities witnessed to the love of God and to the love for others through praxis for liberation and justice for slaves and women, but also through dialogue with different races and creeds, as was evident at Pentecost.

One contemporary example of such liberating praxis, Pentecostal internationalism, a dialogue of nations and rights for the poor, takes place at the *barrio transitorio* (transitory neighborhood) of La Chimba in Antofagasta, northern Chile. There, in a makeshift neighbourhood built by the residents beside the rubbish dump of the city of Antofagasta, lives the Jesuit Felipe Berríos. Berríos has been a figure who has attracted media attention not only because of his success in bringing housing to the poor but also by his lifestyle of identification with the poor. Berríos was the director of a Latin American Jesuit-inspired project of bringing housing to the poor with the help of donors, but also by building those houses together with the Chilean young of a middle-class background and with the help of industry. This housing project, currently present in 16 Latin American countries and inspired by the life lived for the poor of the Chilean Jesuit St Alberto Hurtado, had its greatest realization within the Chilean foundation *Un Techo para Chile*, which literally mobilized millions of citizens in Chile who could aid the cause of the poor. Thus, well-to-do citizens took part in communal meals in which a simple plate of spaghetti (*tallarinada*) was served. They could give a cheque to aid the building of houses for the poor but they had to do so in a communal context in which Fr Berríos, like an Old Testament prophet, would call for their repentance and their solidarity with the world of the poor. In his theological reflections, Berríos called all Chileans, but especially Catholics, to break down prejudice, to let the poor evangelize them, and to rethink concepts and attitudes in order to shape a different society based on the values of the Kingdom of God.[46] The project created a utopian moment in Chilean society, through which Fr Berríos challenged many structures of exclusion and provided a tangible challenge to the Catholic Church. After some public misunderstandings with the powerful and with the Papal Nuncio, Fr Berríos requested a transfer back to Africa where he had been working previously; thus he lived for a couple of years in the Ituri region of the Democratic Republic of Congo. On his return to Chile, he continued his practical theology of liberation, residing with temporary occupants of a rubbish dump in northern Chile, a place that did not have electricity or water. Fr Berríos spoke again of his ongoing learning from the poor and his desire to live among those considered by the nation as 'the nation's rubbish'. At the start, there was no clean water or electricity, and Fr Berríos spoke to journalists from his shack about his own process of becoming a Christian by learning from the poor and the marginalized. By 2020, La Chimba became a challenge to the state as Berríos was interviewed by most of the Chilean media in his own shack made of elements taken from the rubbish dump. Within the pandemic, Berríos, together with his group of co-organizers, created a notebook known as the *libreta solidaria* (solidarity notebook) with which residents of this transient camp were able to go to the local stores and purchase groceries up to US$60 per month, refunded to the local shop owners by the Berríos Foundation. In a single appearance on the Catholic University Television Channel on 10 August 2020, Berríos collected US$3,000 for his community enterprise and linked the nation to a scheme whereby they could buy groceries for people at La Chimba directly from their homes through the internet.

Through these activities that resemble those of NGOs we realize that they are actions of liberating praxis that come out of a theological reflection in which Berríos challenges the market sense that economic activities for profit are enterprises that can, through a 'trickle-down' process, help people to develop themselves. Berríos is only one example among many in which the dignity of the people is supported and realized through an action of dialogue in which a person of one tradition operates the values of the Kingdom together with Christians of other traditions. Ecumenical actions within a country such as Chile, with a tiny minority Buddhist, Hindu or Muslim population, remain an exception in a nation still divided between the traditional majority-Catholic and a growing number of Evangelicals and Pentecostals with a different sense of social justice and the action of Christian communities within the socio-politics of the Kingdom. Berríos has criticized the hierarchy of the Catholic Church, including bishops, priests and nuns, because during the pandemic 'they have been absent from the service of the people, particularly those who suffer'. I have remarked in Chapter 2 and in my own personal reflections that the Archbishop of Santiago was not prominent in the Chilean media during the pandemic, while the Jesuits appeared defending and protecting the dignity of immigrants, those without security or a home, and those who wanted to return to their countries of origin, particularly through the Jesuit Refugee Service.[47]

Notes

1 Arpita Chakraborty, 'Wives as Doorways of Citizenship: Indo-Bangladesh Enclaves and the Repositioning of Gender Relations', in Suzanne Clisby (ed.), *Gender, Sexuality and Identities of the Border-lands*, Abingdon and New York: Routledge, 2020, ch. 11.

2 Bengal was partitioned in 1947 under the Partition of India as East Bengal, part of the newly created Pakistan, and later renamed as East Pakistan. In 1971, East Bengal became the independent country of Bangladesh. While Chakraborty focuses on issues of rights, nationality and the agency of women, the Partition of 1947 and the creation of Bangladesh also had enormous religious implications because of villages and localities inhabited by Muslims and Hindus over centuries; see Mario I. Aguilar, *Interreligious Dialogue and the Partition of India: Hindus and Muslims in Dialogue about Violence and Forced Migration*. London: Jessica Kingsley, 2018.

3 J. Stuart Russell, *Parousia: The New Testament Doctrine of Our Lord's Second Coming*, Grand Rapids, MI: Baker Publishing, 1999.

4 Clodovis Boff, *Theology and Praxis: Epistemological Foundations*, Eugene, OR: Wipf and Stock, 2009.

5 'Introduction' in Hussam S. Timani and Loye Sekihata Ashton (eds), *Post-Christian Interreligious Liberation Theology*, London: Palgrave Macmillan, 2019.

6 Miguel A. De La Torre, *Liberation Theology for Armchair Theologians*, Louisville, KY: Westminster John Knox Press, 2013.

7 Sarah Posner, *Unholy: The Christian Right at the Altar of Donald Trump – Why White Evangelicals Worship at the Altar of Donald Trump*, New York: Random House, 2020.

8 Mario I. Aguilar, *The History of Latin American Theology, II: Theology and Civil Society* and *III: A Theology of the Periphery*, London: SCM Press, 2008.

9 www.rainforestinfo.org.au/Peace/ruether.htm, accessed 31.8.20.

10 Seth Dowland, *Family Values and the Rise of the Christian Right*, Philadelphia, PA: University of Pennsylvania Press, 2018.

11 Miguel A. De La Torre, *The Hope of Liberation in World Religions*, Waco, TX: Baylor University Press, 2008; and Mario I. Aguilar, *Church, Liberation and World Religions: Towards a Christian–Buddhist Dialogue*, London: T&T Clark/Continuum, 2012.

12 Eve Rebecca Parker, 'The Virgin and the Whore – An Interreligious Challenge for Our Times: Exploring the Politics of Religious Belonging with Tamar', *The Ecumenical Review* 71/5, 2019, pp. 693–705; Anderson H. M. Jeremiah, *Hybrid Christianity: Dalit Culture, Identity and Theology*, London: Routledge, 2021; Peniel Rajkumar, *Dalit Theology and Dalit Liberation: Problems, Paradigms and Possibilities*, London: Routledge, 2010; and Rajbharath Patta, 'Towards a Subaltern Theology for India', unpublished PhD thesis, University of Manchester, 2018.

13 See among their works: Marcella Althaus-Reid, *Indecent Theology: Theological Perversions in Sex, Gender and Politics*, Abingdon: Routledge, 2000; Kwok Pui-Lan, *Introducing Asian Feminist Theology*, Sheffield: Sheffield Academic Press, 2002; and Mercy Amba Oduyoye, *Daughters of Anowa: African Women and Patriarchy*, Maryknoll, NY: Orbis, 1998.

14 Mercy Amba Oduyoye, *African Women's Theologies, Spirituality and Healing: Theological Perspectives from the Circle of Concerned African Women Theologians*, New York: Paulist Press, 2019.

15 Aloysius Pieris SJ, *An Asian Theology of Liberation*, London and New York: T&T Clark International, 1988.

16 Aloysius Pieris SJ, *Theologie der Befreiung in Asien: Christentum im Kontext der Armut un der Religionen*, Freiburg im Breisgau: Herder Verlag, 1986.

17 Pieris SJ, *An Asian Theology of Liberation*, ch. 2.

18 Pieris SJ, *An Asian Theology of Liberation*, ch. 8.

19 Ambrose Ih-Ren Mong, *Dialogue Derailed: Joseph Ratzinger's War against Pluralist Theology*, Eugene, OR: Pickwick Publications, 2015.

20 Tissa Balasuriya, *Mary and Human Liberation: The Story and the Text*, Harrisburg, PA: Trinity Press International, 1997.

21 Tissa Balasuriya, *Eucharist and Human Liberation*, Eugene, OR: Wipf and Stock, 2004.

22 Aruna Gnanadason, *Listen to the Women! Listen to the Earth!* Geneva: World Council of Churches, 2005.

23 Aruna Gnanadason, *Creator God in Your Grace, Transform the Earth: An Eco-feminist Ethic of Resistance, Prudence and Care*, Saarbrüken: Lambert Academic Publishing, 2012.

24 Aruna Gnanadason, *With Courage and Compassion: Women and the Ecumenical Movement*, Minneapolis, MN: Fortress Press, 2020, p. 2.

25 Aruna Gnanadason and Musimbi R. A. Kanyoro (eds), *Women, Violence, and Nonviolent Change*, Eugene, OR: Wipf and Stock, 2009.

26 R. S. Sugirtharajah, *Asian Biblical Hermeneutics and Postcolonialism: Contesting the Interpretation*, Sheffield: Sheffield Academic Press, 1999; *Voices from the Margin: Interpreting the Bible in the Third*

World, 25th anniversary edn, Maryknoll, NY: Orbis, 2017; and *Jesus in Asia*, Cambridge, MA: Harvard University Press, 2018.

27 Perry Shaw and Havilah Dharamraj (eds), *Challenging Tradition: Innovation in Advanced Theological Education*, London: Langham Global Library, Langham Parternship UK & Ireland, 2018.

28 Havilah Dharamraj, *Altogether Lovely: A Thematic and Intertextual Reading of the Songs of Songs*, Minneapolis, MN: Fortress Press, 2018.

29 Brian Wintle (gen. ed.), Havilah Dharamraj, Jesudason Baskar Jeyaraj and Paul Swarup (Old Testament eds), Jacob Cherian and Finny Philip (New Testament eds), *South Asia Bible Commentary: A One-volume Commentary on the Whole Bible*, Udaipur, Rajasthan: Open Door Publications, and Carlile: Langham Partership, and Grand Rapids, MI: Zondervan, 2015.

30 Havilah Dharamraj, *A Prophet Like Moses? A Narrative – Theological Reading of the Elijah Stories*, Eugene, OR: Wipf and Stock, 2011.

31 Born in North Sulawesi in 1943, Katoppo died in 2007. She studied at Jakarta Theological Seminary and spoke at the first Asian Theological Conference in Sri Lanka. She was a member of the Ecumenical Association of Third World Theologians (EATWOT).

32 Marianne Katoppo, *Raumanen*, Jakarta: The Lontar Foundation, 2018.

33 Mario I. Aguilar, *Theology, Liberation, Genocide: A Theology of the Periphery*, London: SCM Press, 2009; *The 14th Dalai Lama: Peacekeeping and Universal Responsibility*, London and New York: Routledge, 2021; *Pope Francis: Journeys of a Peacemaker* (forthcoming), and *Liberation Theology, Empathy, and Biographies of Suffering* (forthcoming).

34 Marianne Katoppo, *Compassionate & Free: An Asian Woman's Theology*, Maryknoll, NY: Orbis, 1980.

35 Katoppo, *Compassionate and Free*.

36 Anna Sui Hluan, 'Silence in Translation: Interpreting 1 Corinthians 14:34–35 in Myanmar', unpublished PhD thesis, University of Otago, 2016.

37 Hluan, 'Silence in Translation', abstract.

38 Hluan, 'Silence in Translation', p. 1.

39 Hluan, 'Silence in Translation', p. 7.

40 Hluan, 'Silence in Translation', p. 333.

41 Mark R. Thompson and Eric Vincent C. Batalla (eds), *Routledge Handbook of Contemporary Philippines*, London: Routledge, 2017.

42 Melba Padilla Maggay, *Transforming Society*, London: SPCK, 1994.

43 Melba Padilla Maggay, *Rise Up & Walk: Religion and Culture in Empowering the Poor*, Eugene, OR: Wipf and Stock, 2016.

44 Peter-Ben Smit, *Old Catholic and Philippine Independent Ecclesiologies in History: The Catholic Church in Every Place*, Leiden: Brill, 2011.

45 Teresa Morgan, *Roman Faith and Christian Faith: Pistis and Fides in the Early Roman Empire and Early Churches*, Oxford: Oxford University Press, 2015.

46 Felipe Berríos SJ, *Un techo para Latinoamérica*, Santiago: Aguilar-El Mercurio, 2012.

47 Servicio Jesuita a Migrantes (SJM) at https://sjmchile.org, accessed 31.8.20.

Conclusions: An Interfaith Theology of the Poor

I return to the road to Emmaus where those conversing did not have a great academic seminar but they recognized each other as humans, as human beings on a journey, and finally they recognized the risen Lord in the sharing of food. It is in those moments that we recognize that God is walking with us – when food is shared, hope is spoken and solidarity is realized. The Divine and the Divinity bring together our daily human toil with the realization of heaven for a minute but within the hellish suffering of the poor. After those moments of torture, death and desolation in Jerusalem, the Lord appeared once again to the disciples and brought them consolation. He visited the suffering, desolate and marginalized in order to reiterate the message of the Kingdom of God and the Beatitudes.

The multiplicity of belonging arises not out of the national structures or out of the symbolic structures of belonging to one community, but of an awareness and living of a larger humanity. As I have outlined previously, the Kingdom of God in Christianity provides the opening to a world in which God certainly is larger than our borders and limits, because other-wise she would be limited and would not be God. Thus, our fresh contemporary reflection is not only on the method of liberation theology (praxis), but on its 'truth' (orthopraxis) and its location (belonging).

As in the experience of Jon Sobrino, who lost his Jesuit companions to the guns of the Salvadorian army and to the powerful, 'What we have spoken about here is utopia. But without utopia there is no life.'[1] Within this current post-pandemic utopia, I have proposed that those engaged in a liberating praxis among the poor and the marginalized walk hand in hand with those engaged in the orthopraxy of interreligious dialogue and learn from and live with the poor and the marginalized. The road could be called a liberating interreligious dialogue from the side of the poor and the marginalized; however, such a road only starts with the post-pandemic wave of an interreligious theology of the poor. For, in the sharp analysis of pandemic centres and peripheries, 'we need more than ever to theologize from the world's multiple peripheries amongst, with, for and as the marginalized'.[2] How do we do this? This is the challenge and the utopia after the pandemic, to realize the Kingdom of God. Inshallah!

Notes

1 Jon Sobrino SJ, 'Foreword: With Hope and Gratitude', in Robert Lassale-Klein, *Blood and Ink: Ignacio Ellacuría, Jon Sobrino, and the Jesuit Martyrs of the University of Central America*, Maryknoll, NY: Orbis, 2014.

2 James Harry Morris, 'The Marginalized in the Pandemic Crisis', *The Japan Mission Journal* 74/4, 2020.

Index